The Investor's

Self-Teaching Seminars

INVESTING IN
TAX-SAVING
MUNICIPAL BONDS

*One of a Series of Hands-On Workshops
Dedicated to the Serious Investor*

David L. Scott

PROBUS PUBLISH
Chicago, Illinois

Library of Congress Cataloging in Publication Data Available

ISBN 1-55738-182-8

Printed in the United States of America

BB

1 2 3 4 5 6 7 8 9 0

Additional Titles in
The Investor's Self-Teaching Seminars Series
Available from Probus Publishing

Allocating and Managing Your Investment Assets, Richard Koff

Financial Statement Analysis, Charles J. Woelfel

Investing in High-Yield Stocks, Peter D. Heerwagen

Investing in Rental Properties, Robert W. Richards & Grover C. Richards

Trading Stock Index Options, Mikel T. Dodd

Understanding and Managing Investment Risk & Return, David L. Scott

Understanding and Trading Listed Stock Options, Carl F. Luft & Richard K. Sheiner

Understanding and Using Margin, Michael T. Curley

Understanding the Stock Market, David T. Sutton

Using Technical Analysis, Clifford Pistolese

Calculating, Protecting and Enhancing Your Net Worth, Kevin J. Sears

Understanding and Trading Futures, Carl F. Luft

Your Home as Your Best Investment, Robert W. Richards & Grover C. Richards

Forthcoming Titles

Mutual Fund Switch Strategies and Timing Tactics, Warren Boroson

Insurance As an Investment: Getting the Most for Your Money, Ben G. Baldwin & Maureen M. Baldwin

91–41201

TABLE OF CONTENTS

v

PREFACE

Most people have a thing about taxes—they don't like to pay them. It's not necessarily that these individuals are unpatriotic or dishonest, although some of them undoubtedly skirt the gray areas of the laws. Generally, these are individuals who feel that sending money to the government is like dropping dollar bills from an airplane without knowing for certain who is going to be there to pick up the fluttering greenbacks.

Municipal bonds are an investment vehicle that allow individuals of relatively modest means and with no knowledge of sophisticated tax dodges to reduce legally the amount of money that must be paid to the government. Municipal bonds do not require that a high-powered tax accountant or self-proclaimed investment advisor be hired. They do not require that sophisticated records involving depreciation, maintenance, and incidental expenses be kept. By and large, municipal bonds are an uncomplicated tax-exempt investment.

Even though municipal bonds are a relatively homogeneous and uncomplicated investment, not all municipal bonds are alike. There are differences, sometimes significant differences, of which investors should be aware. Instead of viewing these differences as a hindrance to investing in municipal bonds, they should be considered positive influences that provide investors with added flexibility—flexibility as to maturities, flexibility as to riskiness, and flexibility as to diversity.

Investors interested in purchasing municipal bonds should locate brokers with an interest in these securities that is over and above the self-interest of earning commissions from their sale. Many brokers have a few customers who are interested in municipal bonds, but only a small proportion of brokers make this investment their main area of interest and expertise. The majority of brokers realize that there are substantially more commissions to be earned from customers who trade in stocks, options, and futures contracts than from individuals who purchase twenty-year municipal bonds with the intention of holding them until maturity.

Investing in Tax-Saving Municipal Bonds provides the necessary information to pursue an informed investment policy with respect to municipal bonds. The first order of business, of course, is for investors to decide if municipal bonds are an appropriate investment. By and large, the appropriateness of owning municipal bonds depends on an individual's goals and financial position. Material on the usefulness and appropriateness of municipal bonds is included in the initial two chapters of this book.

The reader also will find descriptions of the various types of municipal bonds that are available for purchase. Municipal securities come in a wide variety of flavors that frequently are categorized in terms of the bonds' issuers. Bonds from different groups of issuers tend to have different characteristics; thus, a general knowledge of bond categories is important.

Individuals who find that municipal bonds are an appropriate investment must decide whether to purchase these securities individually in the primary or secondary markets, or to buy into trusts or investment companies that specialize in municipal bonds and pass tax-exempt interest through to investors. Readers will find information both on building a portfolio of municipal bonds and on comparing mutual funds and unit investment trusts.

Don't overlook the valuable material in the appendices of this book. A discussion of the alternative minimum tax, a guide to the taxation of municipal bonds in each of the fifty states and the District of Columbia, a description of how municipal bonds are brought to market, an explanation of bond ratings, and a selective glossary to clarify municipal bond terminology are all included in the book's final section.

I would like to express a special thank you to Stephanie Bigwood, recent mother, financial advisor, former bond trader, former broker, and one of my favorite former students, for her assistance in this project. Stephanie's expertise and varied experience with municipal bonds has been a great help. She also contributed substantially to the material in Chapter Two.

David L. Scott
Valdosta, Georgia

Chapter
One

WHY INVEST IN MUNICIPAL BONDS?

Little more than a decade ago, the demand for municipal securities derived mostly from financial institutions such as commercial banks and investment companies. Individuals, if they became involved in municipal bonds at all, generally did so by purchasing mutual fund shares or by taking ownership positions in investment trusts packaged by broker-dealers. Even these professionally packaged products remained a mystery to the majority of individual investors. Individuals with large incomes and substantial wealth always had provided a market for underwriters and brokers of municipal bonds, but wealthy investors played the game on a different level than the masses of individual investors.

The early 1980s, the initial years of the Reagan Administration, were ushered in with an investment environment consisting of high interest rates, high marginal income tax rates, and an escalating supply of municipal bonds—conditions that served to reverse the perceptions of many individuals that municipal bonds were only for financial institutions and fat cats. Within a relatively short time, individual issues of municipal bonds in the primary market began flowing directly into the portfolios of individual investors. It was not long until the flow became a torrent. Although both the investment incentives and the number of new issues of municipal bonds diminished following the Tax Reform Act of 1986, municipal securities have continued to increase as a popular investment choice for individual investors who seek to reduce their tax obligations to federal and state treasuries.

THE ATTRACTIVENESS OF MUNICIPAL BONDS

Municipal bonds—whether acquired directly as part of a new issue, in the secondary markets, or indirectly through the purchase of mutual fund shares of investment trusts—possess characteristics that can make them attractive assets to own. As is the case with virtually any type of investment asset, however, municipal bonds are better suited for some individuals that others, because not all investors are able to take full advantage of these securities' desirable attributes. As the most obvious example, it makes little sense for an investor with no tax obligations to purchase tax-advantaged investments. This may state the obvious, but it is not at all unusual for individuals who pay taxes at a relatively low rate to express an interest in municipal bond ownership. Likewise, individuals sometimes ponder the purchase of municipal bonds for individual retirement accounts that already defer income tax liabilities.

The distinguishing feature that gives municipal bonds investment appeal is their tax advantage. In general, interest income derived from the ownership of municipal bonds is free of most taxes, although the tax-free status of these bonds varies somewhat depending upon the peculiarities of an individual bond issue and the legal residence of the investor. Because interest income from municipal bonds generally escapes taxation, an investor can frequently earn a higher after-tax return from a municipal bond than from a regular taxable bond, even though the municipal bond carries a lower rate of interest.

Exhibit 1-1 illustrates the distribution of interest payments for two $1,000 par bonds. The first bond has a 9 percent coupon and pays annual interest of $90. Assuming that the bondholder pays federal taxes of 33 percent, state taxes of 6 percent, and local taxes of 5 percent, the annual tax liability from owning one bond will be $30, $5.40, and $4.50, respectively, leaving the investor with $50.10 to spend. The municipal bond in Exhibit 1-1 has a coupon of 7 percent and pays interest that is not taxable at any governmental

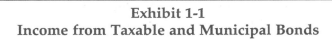

Exhibit 1-1
Income from Taxable and Municipal Bonds

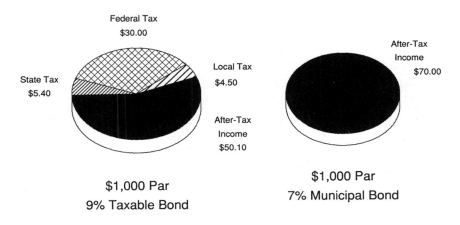

Federal Tax
$30.00

State Tax
$5.40

Local Tax
$4.50

After-Tax
Income
$50.10

$1,000 Par
9% Taxable Bond

After-Tax
Income
$70.00

$1,000 Par
7% Municipal Bond

level. Thus, the investor is able to keep the entire $70 annual interest payment. Even though the municipal bond pays a lower before-tax return than the taxable security, the investor is better off owning the municipal bond than the taxable bond .

The tax implications of owning municipal bonds will be discussed later in this chapter and again in Chapter 3, but it is important to understand at the beginning that an investor's effective tax rate is a crucial consideration in making an intelligent decision on whether to purchase municipal bonds. The higher an individual's effective tax rate, the more likely municipal bonds are a good investment choice. Individuals with minimal tax liabilities generally should avoid municipal bonds.

The steady stream of tax-free income produced by municipal bonds is another attribute that is especially appealing to someone who desires current investment income as opposed to capital appreciation. This is an important consideration, because there is a strong probability that if current income is a low priority, an investor will be better off concentrating on investments other than bonds. This is true whether the bonds are taxable or tax- free. Thus, for the majority of investors, the desire for a steady source of current income is just as important as a high marginal tax rate when considering whether to invest in municipal bonds.

Another investment advantage to municipal bonds is their safety. Investment advisors and professional investors generally view municipal bonds as one of the more secure investment alternatives. In general, issuers of municipal bonds faithfully have met both their interest and principal obligations in full and on time. On the negative side, there is some reason to believe that the increasing debt burdens taken on by the many issuers of these bonds, coupled with the trend toward issuing bonds backed by the revenues from specific projects as opposed to general tax revenues, are reasons for investor concern. The history of limited defaults on municipal issues also must be viewed in light of the fact that the United States has not experienced a major economic downturn since many of the currently outstanding bonds were issued. An expanded discussion of the risks that are incurred by owners of municipal bonds is found in Chapter 4.

WHERE MUNICIPAL BONDS ORIGINATE

Municipal bonds are issued by a variety of political entities that, for one reason or another, find themselves needing an infusion of outside funds. These political entities borrow for the same reasons that corporations and individuals do, but differences exist in the timing and in the amounts of income and spending flows. In the case of municipal issuers, the normal revenue stream consists of various taxes and user fees. In the case of corporations, on the other hand, revenue comes from sales. And, in the case of individuals, the revenue comes from wages and investments. Instead of paying for the construction of factories, household appliances, and for occasional vacations, municipal expenditures must provide for bridges, water plants, rapid transit systems, airport terminals, and roads, in addition to wages and other operating expenses.

Locating a Lender

Like any intelligent borrower, the appointed or elected managers of a municipality attempt to locate the lender that offers the best terms on a loan. In some instances this lender may be a commercial bank, in which case the municipality may negotiate a loan directly with a single lending institution. In other instances, especially when substantial amounts of long-term borrowing are required to support very expensive capital projects, the municipality may find that the best way to generate funds is by offering public bonds in the capital markets.

If a municipality opts to raise funds through a public bond issue, it generally employs the services of an investment banker to assist in setting the terms of the issue, taking care of the legal details, and locating buyers for the bonds. Investment bankers are in the business of providing assistance to public and private organizations that need to raise funds in the capital markets, a job for which most industrial and government organizations are not prepared. Investment bankers are able to provide advice and raise the required funds on more favorable terms than most municipalities could by going it alone. In many instances, the investment banker actually underwrites an issue by purchasing the securities from the municipality and reselling them to investors. The eventual buyers of the municipality's bonds may turn out to be banks, investment companies, and/or individual investors. For additional details on how municipalities bring securities to market see Appendix E.

There is nothing inherently wrong with borrowing funds to bridge temporary revenue shortfalls or to finance unusually large capital projects that are expected to provide public benefits over an extended period of time. Borrowing tens of millions of dollars to finance a water plant that will generate both benefits and revenues over several decades is not necessarily a case of deceitful finance. Nevertheless, when borrowed funds are used to pay for recurring operating expenses such as wages and utilities, financial difficulties may be on the horizon.

Municipal bonds held by investors represent creditor claims by the bondholder on the issuer. The issuer is obligated to repay the principal on a specific date and, generally, to make semi-annual interest payments to the owner of the bond. Payment of both interest and principal is a legal obligation of the borrower that can be enforced by the bondholders in the courts. Bonds contrast with shares of common or preferred stock that represent ownership claims in that it is not possible to acquire shares of ownership in cities, states, or public utility districts (at least, not legally) and no common stock is issued by these municipal entities.

Municipal Bonds in the Secondary Market

Investors who purchase municipal bonds in the primary market do not have the right to sell these bonds back to the issuers (there are a few exceptions), but the bondholders are free to resell the securities to other investors. As is the case with virtually all securities, municipal bonds can be transferred at negotiated prices. Depending upon what occurs with respect to market rates of interest and the ability of the issuer to make the required payments subsequent to the date of the original issue, the bonds may resell in the secondary market at a price that is different than the original issue price.

The secondary market for municipal bonds is found in the over-the-counter market (OTC) rather than in the organized exchanges such as the New York Stock Exchange. The OTC is comprised of security dealers who are in the business of buying and selling securities via computer and telephone. Some of these dealers specialize in common stocks, while others deal in bonds. Thus, a municipal bond dealer stands ready to purchase municipal bonds that investors wish to sell and to sell municipal bonds that investors may wish to purchase. Most investors contact dealers through regular brokerage firms although, in many instances, the broker also may act as a dealer (thus the term *broker-dealer*) and stand ready to buy or sell individual issues of municipal bonds for his or her own account.

All of the provisions that apply to the original purchaser of a municipal bond transfer automatically to the subsequent owner of the bond. Thus, items detailed at the time of original sale such as the amount and dates of interest payments, the maturity date, the call date and call price, and specific collateral pledged to the bondholder, applies to any subsequent purchaser who acquires bonds in the secondary market. Unlike the warranties issued by many manufacturers of appliances and automotive replacement parts, the issuer of a municipal bond enters into a contract that is freely and automatically transferable to a new owner of the security.

Because municipal bonds routinely trade in the secondary market after the date of original issue, it makes little difference whether an individual purchases bonds as part of a new issue or acquires the securities in the secondary market. One consideration for investors weighing purchases in either the primary or secondary markets is that selling commissions on new issues (e.g., securities traded in the primary market) are absorbed by the issuer so that there are no selling fees charged to buyers. Brokerage fees are charged to both buyers and sellers in the secondary market although these commissions nearly always are concealed in the bid and ask prices quoted by brokers.

CHARACTERISTICS OF MUNICIPAL BONDS

The term *municipal bond* generally is used as a generic term to include any bond that has been issued by a state, city, or some other political entity beneath the federal level. Thus, a broker's recommendation to purchase for specific municipal bonds might include an issue by the State of Massachusetts or an issue from the Metropolitan Atlanta Rapid Transit Authority (MARTA). Neither of these bonds is used by a municipal government in the strict sense that the issuer is a city or town, but both bonds are considered municipal issues.

Until the mid-1980s, the term *municipal bond* was synonymous with virtually any debt security that paid interest that was not subject to federal taxation. However, tax reform in 1986 muddied the distinctness by creating a new category of municipal securities that pay interest that *is* subject to federal taxation. Tax reform also created another class of municipal bonds that pay interest that *may* be subject to special federal taxation depending upon the individual investor's financial status with respect to items such as tax shelters and amounts and sources of income. Chapter 5 and Appendix D amply demonstrate that tax reform made the world of municipal bond investing considerably more confusing. Despite these recently introduced complications relative to taxation, the fundamentals of municipal bonds are essentially the same as for other long-term debt obligations.

Interest Payments

Virtually all municipal bonds make semi-annual interest payments that are based upon two factors: the principal amount, or face value of the bond, and the coupon rate of interest that is specified at the time of issue. Thus, the owner of a $1,000 principal amount, 8 percent coupon bond will receive annual interest of $80 ($1,000 x .08) in the form of two $40 semi-annual payments. The owner of ten of these bonds will receive an interest income of $400 ($40 x 10) every six months. The dollar amount of a bond's interest payments remains constant, regardless of changes in market rates of interest from the time the bond is issued until the bond is redeemed by the issuer. Subsequent changes in market rates of interest will affect the market value of bonds with a fixed coupon rate, but not the dollar amount of interest that the bonds pay to their owners. Fixed interest payments cause municipal bonds to vary in value in response to fluctuations in market rates of interest.

An investor who purchases a municipal bond between interest payment dates is required to reimburse the seller for the interest that has accrued on the bond since the last interest payment was made. Thus, buying a bond two months after the last interest payment (i.e., four months prior to the next interest payment) will require that the buyer pay the seller for the two months of interest that accrued on the bond since the last payment date (but which the bondholder has not received). The buyer will be reimbursed for this additional payment to the seller when a check for the entire six months of interest is received on the interest payment date (two months of the six months of interest will represent payment for a period when the bond was not held by the new owner).

Although somewhat rare, there are both taxable and nontaxable bonds paying interest that can change between the issue date and maturity. Depending upon the specifics detailed in the indenture agreement, a change in interest payments may be a one-time event, or adjustments may occur periodically throughout the life of the bond. The volatility of market interest rates in the 1970s and 1980s produced investor demand for issues of bonds with interest payments that change to reflect existing levels of short-term interest rates at specified intervals. Changing interest payments and other variations on standard fixed-coupon municipal bonds are discussed in more detail in Chapter 4.

Virtually all municipal bond issuers pay interest by check directly to bondholders or, when bonds are being held in a brokerage account, to the brokerage firm which then credits the investor's account. The procedure for making interest payments on municipal bonds is consistent with the practice used by other bond issuers. There are, of course, some exceptions. For example, beginning in the early 1980s issuers and investment bankers sold some issues at deep discounts to par value. These bonds accrue interest during the time the bond is outstanding. Thus, rather than the bondholder receiving semi-annual checks or account credits, the bond gradually accumulates interest over its lifetime until maturity; the security carries an accreted value that is equal to the face value at which the bond is redeemed. These bonds—termed *zero-coupon bonds*—are the exception rather than the rule in the world of municipal bonds although they offer some very important advantages (and, as always, disadvantages) over ordinary bonds that make periodic interest payments. Zero-coupon bonds are discussed in more detail in Chapter 2.

Principal

Unlike most corporate bonds that nearly always are denominated in $1,000 principal amounts, municipal bonds normally are denominated in $5,000 principal amounts. Because of the $5,000 denomination, the minimum investment in the municipal bond market is $5,000 with additional purchases made in $5,000 increments. Many investors find this relatively large minimum investment a serious impediment to purchasing individual securities because a diversified portfolio of eight to ten different municipal bond issues requires a fairly hefty amount of personal funds and may take quite some time to acquire. These problems can be overcome by indirectly acquiring municipal bonds through the purchase of either mutual funds or investment trusts that limit their holdings to tax-exempt securities. Tax-exempt mutual funds and unit trusts are discussed in Chapter 6.

Maturities

At the date of issue, municipal bond maturities range from a matter of weeks to thirty or more years. Even single bond issues frequently have a wide range of available maturities so that investors purchasing municipal bonds that are part of a new issue have little difficulty locating securities with desirable maturities. In the secondary market in which previously issued bonds are traded among investors, bonds with a wide variety of maturity lengths are generally available, although the inventory of bonds with a particular broker-dealer may be limited.

Between the new issues of municipal bonds that constantly flow through the primary market and the huge number of bond issues that trade in the secondary market, an investor should be able to obtain bonds with virtually any maturity as long as there is some flexibility as to the issuer. Thus, if there are no fifteen-year bonds of a particular issuer available in either the primary or the secondary markets, there are likely to be fifteen-year bonds available from another issuer with similar risk and return characteristics.

Redemptions Prior to Maturity

The scheduled maturities of municipal bonds are not always what they seem. The fact is that many municipal bonds do not remain outstanding until their maturity because the issuers are permitted, under certain circumstances, to repurchase the bonds prior to the scheduled maturity. Unfortunately for investors, the conditions under which early redemptions are implemented nearly always favor the issuers. A large proportion of municipal bonds are subject to these early redemptions.

Many bond indenture agreements permit a municipality to pay off an existing bond issue with the proceeds of a new bond issue. This financial operation, called a *refunding,* is employed during periods of low interest rates when borrowers are able to replace old, high-interest outstanding bonds with new low-interest bonds. A municipality undertakes a refunding in order to reduce its interest expense. The investor holding the existing bonds must sell the securities back to the issuer at a time when funds generated by the sale can be reinvested only at a significantly lower return than was earned on the called bonds.

While many municipal bonds may be called prior to their stated maturities, a stipulated period of protection from an early redemption generally is included in the agreement between the issuer and the investor. Thus, a bond with a thirty-year maturity may not be callable by the issuer during the initial ten years following the date of issue. It is important to note that the period of call protection begins with the date of issue; thus, investors acquiring a bond in the secondary market may have no protection from an early call by the issuer. For example, an investor purchasing the bond noted above fifteen years after the date of issue would receive no protection from an early redemption, as the period of protection terminated five years prior to the transaction. The possibility of early redemption is a very important consideration for investor, and information relevant to a possible call should be obtained prior to purchasing a municipal bond.

Safety

The promise of principal and interest on most municipal bonds is considered to be reliable. Payments to municipal bond holders are not as certain as are the principal and interest from U.S. Treasury securities, of course, as Treasuries are in a safety classification all their own. Even though municipal bonds taken as a class are considered relatively safe, the possibility of loss can vary significantly among different bond issues, and it is certainly not unheard of for an issuer to default on a bond issue.

The most spectacular example of a municipal default was the Washington Public Power Supply System (WPPSS, pronounced "woops") which terminated payments on the $2.25 billion principal amount of its obligations. This largest ever municipal default resulted in nearly a complete loss for many of the system's bondholders. It is possible for cities, hospitals, airports, and virtually any governmental body or business entity to be unable to pay their bills. Thus, there is always some chance that an issuer will be unable to make the contractual payments stated in a bond agreement.

There are other kinds of risk that can result in significant losses for municipal bond investors. For example, long-term municipal bonds fluctuate in price as market rates of interest change. Thus, there is a real possibility that an investor will lose a substantial portion of his or her investment if it is necessary to sell a bond prior to maturity. Likewise, the municipal bond investor may find that the purchasing power of both interest payments and principal are eaten away by rampant inflation. These and other risks will be discussed fully in Chapter 4.

One relatively new development relating to the safety of holding municipal bonds is the increasing use of outside guarantors who promise that payments of interest and principal will take place. Issuers will sometimes purchase the guarantee from commercial banks that issue letters of credit guaranteeing payments to bondholders as scheduled. More frequently, issuers purchase insurance from firms established to insure this particular risk. Outside guarantors strengthen the bondholder's position because with the guarantee two organizations are promising payment; the issuer continues to have the primary responsibility and the insurer assumes the responsibility if the issuer is unable to fulfill the terms of the contract.

Fortunately, it is possible for an informed investor to select municipal bonds in such a way that the risk of loss is minimized. Risks to municipal bondholders include the potential loss of income and the reduction in market value that occurs when an issuer's ability to make interest payments and/or principal repayments is impaired, and the loss that can occur if municipal bonds must be sold prior to their scheduled maturity.

THE TAX ASPECTS OF MUNICIPAL BONDS

There is no getting around the fact that people buy municipal bonds primarily because they pay interest that is free of taxation. Unlike many tax-advantaged investments that merely defer taxes or that produce expenses that can be utilized to offset income earned from other sources, most municipal bonds produce income that is not taxed.

Actually, municipal bonds have the potential of producing two distinct kinds of income: income from interest payments and income (or losses) from changes in market value. Income from interest payments is free of taxation, but gains caused by rising bond values are taxable in the periods in which the gains are realized through a sale. In the taxation of realized capital gains, municipal bonds are treated like any other capital asset.

Because avoiding taxes is the main reason to invest in municipal bonds, one needs to understand exactly what tax liabilities may be affected by owning municipal bonds. The advantages of investing in municipal bonds can vary considerably, depending upon an individual's taxable income and place of residence.

Federal Income Taxes

Most municipal bonds make interest payments that are entirely free of the federal income tax. The exemption from federal taxation applies to most municipal bond interest regardless of an individual's marginal tax rate or the amounts of other income received. A limited number of municipal bonds pay interest that is either subject to regular federal income taxes (called *taxable municipal bonds*) or to the alternative minimum tax (AMT). Bonds falling within either of these two categories are relatively rare and always are identified in offering statements and by brokers as being subject to taxation or the possibility of taxation. The difference in either actual or potential taxation is very important, because bonds that may be subject to any taxation are less valuable and will trade at reduced prices to produce higher yields compared to municipal bonds that pay interest completely free of taxation. Chapter 2 offers a more complete examination of taxable municipal bonds, and Appendix D gives an expanded look at the alternative minimum tax.

The exemption of interest payments from federal taxation is of crucial importance because the federal income tax is the levy that, for the majority of investors, produces the highest tax bills and the highest marginal tax rate. States and municipalities, if they tax income at all, generally set their highest marginal rates at 10 percent or below. The federal government, on the other hand, currently has a maximum marginal tax rate of 31 percent. Even this comparatively high marginal rate is down significantly from the 50 percent marginal rate that existed at the beginning of the 1980s and marginal rates of between 70 and 92 percent that were in force several decades earlier.

State Income Taxes

Potential tax savings at the state level resulting from owning municipal bonds depend upon the tax code of the particular state where an investor resides. Some states, including Alaska, Connecticut, Florida, Nevada, and New Hampshire, do not tax individual income so that, from the standpoint of avoiding state income taxes, residents have little incentive to own municipal bonds. Other states, including New York and California, levy taxes on personal income at or near double-digit rates. Residents of these states can realize substantial savings on state income taxes by investing in municipal bonds that qualify for the exemption.

Most states that levy a tax on individual income do not tax the interest income from municipal bonds issued within the state. For example, Georgia assesses a state income tax that reaches a maximum of 6 percent, but the tax is not levied against the interest income from municipal bonds issued within the state. Georgia does, however, require its residents to pay taxes on interest from municipal bonds issued outside Georgia. Thus, if a Georgia resident holds bonds issued by the state of California, he or she must report the interest payments from the bonds as income. Such a policy influences investors to purchase municipal bonds issued within their respective home states. The interest income from these bonds is exempted from taxation to create incentives for residents to purchase local bonds.

A limited number of states that impose an income tax do not tax the interest that is paid on any municipal bond. For example, Indiana has a state income tax but exempts the interest income of municipal bonds from taxation no matter where the issuer is located. Residents of states that exempt all municipal bond interest from taxation offer the investor little incentive to limit holdings to municipal bonds issued within their respective states. In fact, the ability to geographically diversify a municipal bond portfolio without suffering a tax penalty is a significant benefit of residing in one of these states.

A few states do not exempt any municipal bond interest from taxation whether the bonds are issued within or outside the state. For example, Illinois taxes the interest that investors receive from municipal bonds in exactly the same manner that it taxes the interest payments from corporate bonds. This taxation applies to municipals issued within Illinois as well as to municipals issued outside the state. Such a tax policy eliminates the incentive for concentrating on municipals within a given state at the same time that it reduces somewhat the desirability of all municipals.

Intangible Taxes

An intangible tax is a levy against the market value of an asset rather than against realized increases in value or income produced by the asset. Thus, an investor is required to pay a tax that is determined by the market value of the asset on a specified date at the tax rate established by the taxing district. An intangible tax is levied by some states and by some local governments. In some instances, the tax is levied by a local government but collected by the state.

As a rule, intangible taxes are not levied on municipal bonds issued within the state. For example, residents of Georgia are not required to pay an intangible tax on the value of municipal bonds issued within the state. On the other hand, the Georgia intangible tax does apply to municipal bonds issued outside Georgia.

The intangible tax is generally quite small, typically one-tenth of one percent of the market value; thus, the tax is not an important consideration when putting together a portfolio of municipal securities. In many states, the tax historically has been widely evaded by investors and spottily enforced by taxing authorities. Some critics contend that most states that have an intangible tax spend more money attempting to enforce the tax than they take in from the tax.

Local Income Taxes

Taxation of income by local governments is not widespread, but, in localities where the tax is levied, it can be an important consider-

---

Exhibit 1-2
A Municipal Investor's Tax Checklist

Each state has unique laws regarding the taxation of municipal bond income. Investors who are interested in acquiring municipal bonds first should determine how their state levies taxes against these securities. An investor must understand the following items prior to investing in municipal bonds.

Y/N

Interest on in-state municipals is taxed by state _____
Interest on out-of-state municipals is taxed by state _____
Interest on in-state municipals is taxed by local authorities _____
Interest on out-of-state municipals is taxed by local authorities _____
Intangible tax applies to in-state municipals _____
Intangible tax applies to out-of-state municipals _____

---

ation for investors. As a rule, local taxing authorities exempt the interest from bonds issued by the authority or within the state in which the local authority operates. As is the case with taxation at the state level, the degree of taxation and the types of income that are and are not taxed at the local level vary extensively according to local codes. To be an informed investor one must determine the extent to which municipal bond income and values are taxed by the applicable state and local authorities. Exhibit 1-2 provides a simple tax checklist for investors who are considering the purchase of municipal bonds.

Chapter
Two

THE VARIETY OF MUNICIPAL BONDS

The municipal bonds issued and traded in the secondary market can be classified in a number of different ways. For example, municipal bonds can be categorized in terms of type of issuer, nature of the guarantee, length of the maturity, or taxability of interest payments. This chapter will examine the wide variety of municipal bonds available for purchase.

ISSUERS OF MUNICIPAL BONDS

As mentioned in Chapter 1, the term *municipal bond* tends to be used in a generic manner and applied to any public bond issue, be it a debt security issued by a state, an airport, or a public hospital (but not the federal government). Most investors are under the impression that municipal bonds pay interest that is free of federal income taxes, but some municipal interest is taxable.

Because of the assorted nature of public organizations, there are numerous and diverse public institutions that borrow funds through the issuance of municipal bonds. This first section of Chapter 2 examines some of the common categories of these issuers and some of the features of their securities.

States, Cities, Towns, and Counties

Bonds issued by states, cities, towns, and counties usually are general obligations of the issuer. General obligation bonds are backed by the full faith and credit and, therefore, the full taxing power of the issuer. For example, the holder of a New York state general obligation bond is able to look to all of the tax revenues that New York can raise to pay the bond's interest and principal as they come due. The main sources of tax revenues for most states consist of corporate and personal income taxes and sales taxes, although certainly many other types of tax revenues, as well as federal revenue sharing programs, exist. The programs of taxation available to states, cities, towns, and counties are powerful tools for raising funds, thus giving the owners of general obligation bonds a relatively strong claim to repayment.

Just as New York State can implement new taxes or raise the taxes that are already in place in order to generate revenues to meet its bond and other financial obligations, it also can take steps to reduce certain expenses. Baltimore, Maryland, is an example of a municipality that chose the latter approach to government financial management. When faced with a possible budget deficit approaching $50 million for the 1990 fiscal year, Baltimore's mayor announced a plan to slash between 800 and 1,000 city jobs. This sort of fiscal restraint is an approach that some municipal governments might choose in order to preserve the fiscal soundness of the annual budget and the municipality's financial reserves.

Bonds issued by counties are supported primarily by property taxes on real property, e.g., private residences and business properties. Consider Forsyth County, North Carolina, the home of many large companies and major operating divisions. Hanes Knitwear, First Wachovia Corporation, U.S. Air, R. J. Reynolds Company, Integon Corporation, Wake Forest University, and several hospitals and trucking, textile, and furniture concerns have a major presence in this county. Such a diversified and substantial base of employers tends to promote a stable environment for the collection of property taxes, which in turn should provide considerable comfort to an investor contemplating purchasing a Forsyth County, North Carolina, general obligation bond.

When a professional credit analyst evaluates the financial strength of a general obligation bond issued by a state, city, town, or county, he or she considers many different factors. Instead of evaluating the fiscal merits of a multitude of municipal entities, most individual investors look to the credit ratings assigned by the large bond rating houses. Credit ratings for municipal bonds are discussed in more length in Chapter 4 and descriptions of particular ratings are provided in Appendix A.

School District Bonds

A school district bond is normally a general obligation of the county in which the school district is located. The separate category exists merely to identify the purpose for which the monies are being borrowed. As a rule, school district bonds are considered to be of good quality, although the ability of a community to service debt can vary considerably. The economic strength and diversity of the county guaranteeing repayment of a municipal bond issue are crucial ingredients in determining the quality of the guarantee.

Water and Sewer Revenue Bonds

Water and sewer bonds are issued to support the most basic of municipal services. The monies used to cover the required interest and principal payments on water and sewer revenue bonds are derived from the collection of water and sewerage bills. Professionals in the field of municipal finance feel that, taken as a group, water and sewer revenue bonds are relatively low risk municipal securities because of the absolute necessity for the product and service that guarantee payment on the securities. Nevertheless, holders of water and sewer bonds cannot usually look to other sources of revenue, such as tax receipts or revenues from other municipal projects or services, to obtain payment on water and sewer bonds in the event that the bond issuer defaults. Thus, even high-quality revenue bonds guaranteed by a relatively secure source of repayment generally are considered to be somewhat inferior to most general obligation bonds.

EXHIBIT 2-1
Municipal Bonds with "Double" Guarantees

Some water bonds are backed by a local government's promise of payment as well as by the revenues collected from water and sewerage fees. For example, Washington Suburban Sanitary District (WSSD) bonds are repaid with water bill payments, but the obligations are also backed by the full faith and credit of Montgomery County, Maryland, and Prince George's County, Maryland. Thus, WSSD bonds have a "double backing" and are perceived by investors as even safer than general obligation bonds.

Hospital Revenue Bonds and
Nursing Facility Revenue Bonds

In contrast to the relative safety of water and sewer revenue bonds, hospital revenue bonds are in a category that is often considered to contain some of the most risky revenue bonds. The primary source for repayment of hospital bonds is the revenue stream of the issuer, and it is no secret that some hospitals have experienced considerable financial pressure because of increased competition, changes in reimbursement practices on the part of Medicare and private insurers, and other industry trends such as nursing shortages, more outpatient treatments, shorter hospital stays, and the need for expensive equipment designed for special uses.

Because of the questionable financial strength of hospitals, many investment managers recommend that investors steer clear of hospital bonds unless extensive credit research is undertaken prior to investing, or unless the bonds are insured by a strong insurance company or backed by a bank letter of credit. Although some hospitals are fiscally strong, in the case of an industry with such an uncertain future, it is better to be safe than sorry.

Nursing care facilities are in some respects similar to hospitals. For example, both types of facilities are influenced strongly by constantly changing government regulations and insurance reimbursement practices. There seems to be a higher incidence of loss

---

EXHIBIT 2-2
Hospital Revenue Bonds: An Illustration

In order to raise the necessary funds for the purchase of new equipment and for the renovation and construction of facilities, the Hospital Authority of Columbus, Georgia, issued $12,235,000 of tax-exempt revenue anticipation certificates in 1987. To obtain a lower interest cost on the issue, the Authority purchased a municipal bond insurance policy from Bond Investors Guaranty Insurance Company (BIG). The policy obligated the insurance company to pay any principal and interest due on the certificates that remained unpaid by the Authority. Because of the insurance that guaranteed payment to bondholders, Moody's rated the certificates Aaa and Standard & Poor's rated them AAA. Both of these ratings indicate that the rating agencies considered the bonds to be among the safest investment-grade bonds available to investors.

Coupons on the serial bonds ranged from 5.75 percent for bonds maturing in 1990 to 7.50 percent for $595,000 principal amount of bonds maturing in 1998. Term certificates maturing in 2001 carried an 8 percent coupon, and $6 million of term certificates maturing in 2007 were sold at 99.5 percent of par with a coupon of 8.25 percent.

---

associated with bonds issued by nursing care facilities, however, and special caution should be exercised in the analysis of credit risk for this second category of bonds.

Water and sewer issues represent the most basic kind of revenue bond while hospital and nursing facility issues perhaps represent the highest level of credit risk. What categories of bond issuers subject municipal bond investors to a degree of risk that is between these two extremes?

Transportation Bonds

Transportation bonds generally are issued to finance the construction or renovation of roads, bridges, and tunnels. The revenues that are used to pay the interest and principal on the bonds typically come from tolls paid by the users of these facilities. As a result, the relative safety of transportation bonds is a function of just how essential the facility being financed is to its potential users.

A turnpike in Florida spans much of the length of the state. Users are required to pay a toll that is based upon the distance traveled—the distance between the entrance point and exit point. This turnpike is the route of preference for many people; it is strategically located so that it offers the shortest route between many areas. Other individuals, however, might choose other routes so as to avoid paying the turnpike's toll.

The moral to this story is that it is important for an investor to assess the level of essentialness of any given transportation facility before acquiring bonds that are issued to finance the facility's construction or renovation. The investor should study any alternative

---

Exhibit 2-3
Building a Toll Bridge

The William Preston Lane, Jr. Memorial Bridge spans the Chesapeake Bay between Sandy Point (in Anne Arundel County, on Maryland's western shore) and Kent Island on Maryland's famous eastern shore. Before this bridge—nicknamed the Chesapeake Bay Bridge—was constructed, travelers wishing to cross the Chesapeake Bay had two choices: a time-consuming and sometimes rough ferry ride or a very long and tiring (if scenic) drive up one side of the Chesapeake Bay and down the other.

Traffic across the Bay is quite heavy, and the bridge has not only received a great deal of use, but it has, no doubt, been a real boon to the economy on both sides of the Chesapeake Bay. The toll revenue stream in the case of the Chesapeake Bay Bridge appears secure. Not only are alternatives to the bridge time-consuming, but they may not be very cost-efficient given today's high gasoline prices and the extra fuel required to make the long drive around the Chesapeake Bay.

---

facilities that may compete with the transportation facility being considered to ascertain that enough users will pay to utilize the facility and generate the stream of revenues that will service and retire the bond issue in a timely fashion. In the case of the Florida toll road, the steady stream of visitors to the state's East Coast doubtlessly increases the fiscal viability of the turnpike.

Investors should remember that the bonds issued to finance transportation facilities normally remain solely the obligation of the state authorities that have been formed for these specific purposes, and the bonds are supported only by toll revenues that are paid to use the facilities that the bonds have been used to finance. Transportation bonds normally are *not* the general obligation of a state or county, nor are they supported by any tax revenues. In the event that a state or other municipal government chooses to back any particular revenue bond issue (as is the case with the water revenue bond discussed in Exhibit 2-1), the extra guarantee will be reflected both in the official offering statement and in the credit rating assigned to the bond issue.

Airport Revenue Bonds

Airport revenue bonds are issued for the construction, expansion, or refurbishment of an airport (terminal, hanger, and/or runways). An investor must gauge the need and financial viability of the airport and the specific facilities being constructed before feeling confident about investing in bonds that are backed by revenues from the project. Note that in many instances, airport revenue bonds are guaranteed by the lease obligations of a particular airline so that the credit quality of the airline is the major factor influencing the credit quality of the bonds.

Stadium Authority Revenue Bonds

Stadium authority revenue bonds are issued for the construction, expansion, or refurbishment of a sports stadium facility. Because many city boosters feel that organized professional sports contribute to the economic vitality of a city, county, or region, stadium

---

Exhibit 2-4
Airport Revenue Bonds: An Illustration

Charlotte, North Carolina, Special Facility Revenue Bonds backed by a lease agreement with Piedmont Aviation (later acquired by US Air) were issued in 1986 to provide funds for airport terminal construction. The bonds carried a BBB rating (the lowest possible rating to qualify the issues as investment-grade) by both the major rating agencies.

The Tax Reform Act of 1986 stipulated that airport facility bonds, in which more than 10 percent of the proceeds benefit a private party, be subject to the alternative minimum tax (AMT). Because the proceeds from these bonds did benefit a private party—Piedmont Aviation—buyers of the bonds were required to include interest from the securities in consideration for determining if the alternative minimum tax was applicable. Because municipal bonds with interest subject to the AMT are considered less desirable than municipal bonds with interest that is not subject to the alternative minimum tax, these Special Facility Revenue Bonds were issued with relatively high coupons.

---

authorities sometimes are formed to issue tax-exempt bonds provided that the securities satisfy certain requirements.

When contemplating the purchase of a stadium authority revenue bond, an investor should ascertain the final credit behind the issue. In some instances, the city or state may back the issue, while in other cases, stadium authority bonds are guaranteed only by the revenues that the stadium produces. Because of the uncertain economic viability of sports stadiums—despite the hoopla created by the franchise owners, surrounding businesses, and other interested parties—it is a good idea for most investors to avoid issues that are backed only by stadium revenues.

Certain stadium authority issues may not carry tax-exempt status, as is the case with some of the bonds issued recently by the Maryland Stadium Authority for construction of the new baseball complex at Camden Yards in downtown Baltimore. Taxable municipal bonds are discussed in a later section of this chapter.

Housing Authority Mortgage Revenue Bonds

Often a housing authority will be formed to facilitate the financing of homes, especially for first-time home buyers. These public bodies are established by the city, county, or state in which the authorities operate for the express purpose of borrowing funds (i.e., issuing bonds) that are then loaned to home buyers at a slightly higher interest rate than the rate being paid on the bond issue. The credit quality of these issues generally is high because the home buyers are required to make a substantial down payment on the home being financed. If the borrowers do not have sufficient funds for a down payment, credit insurance generally is required to make up the shortfall in the equity position for the property being financed. Thus, even in the event of foreclosure, credit losses on the part of the housing authority usually are nominal.

Authorities involved in single family mortgage programs also frequently have multi-family housing programs that allow builders of apartment complexes, for example, to borrow funds to finance the construction of multi-family projects. The creditworthiness of multi-family housing projects is a function of each "deal" being financed, so that the bond investor should be familiar with the specific project being constructed before acquiring bonds backed by revenues that are generated by the project. When a project is in the construction phase, bonds may have a higher risk because of possible cost overruns or other problems that may not yet be anticipated.

Multi-family housing bond issues often are brought to market with additional credit support, i.e., credit insurance from a large municipal bond insurance company such as MBIA, AMBAC, FGIC, or BIG; a letter of credit from a major bank; or GNMA securities pledged as collateral for the bond issue. Any of these additional credit supports will provide substantial comfort to the investing community and will secure a better reception for the bonds in the marketplace. As a result, credit enhancement generally will enable bond issues to be sold at a reduced rate of interest. Interest payments on multi-family mortgage bonds may or may not be exempt

---

Exhibit 2-5
Examining a Typical Housing Authority Issue

In 1984, the California Housing Finance Agency issued $300 million of home mortgage revenue bonds. The issue included $54 million in serial bonds that matured in six-month intervals beginning August 1, 1986; $230 million in term bonds that matured in the years 1996, 1998, 2004, and 2016; and $16 million in long-term zero-coupon bonds. All of the bonds were payable only from the revenues, assets, and properties pledged under the indenture applicable to this particular issue. The official statement made clear that the bonds were not obligations of the state of California or of any of California's subdivisions other than the agency that issued them.

The bonds were issued to provide funds for the purchase of mortgage loans secured by first mortgages on single family homes, condominiums, units of planned unit developments, and permanently attached manufactured housing. The loans had to be originated and serviced by qualified California lenders. The Agency set a limit on the household income for borrowers and each loan was required to be insured by a private mortgage insurer.

---

from the alternative minimum tax (AMT), a topic discussed in Appendix D.

Another important consideration with regard to single and multi-family housing involves the possibility that the securities may be subject to extraordinary calls. An extraordinary call means that a bond can be called or redeemed, either partially or completely, at any time. Extraordinary calls most frequently occur due to prepayments made by one or more mortgage borrowers. A borrower might prepay a mortgage for any number of reasons—to refinance the loan after a decline in interest rates, to reduce the amount owed on the loan, or because the home being mortgaged was sold.

Extraordinary calls also can occur when market rates of interest drop rapidly after a bond issue comes to market but before the housing authority can lend out the monies raised through the issue. Because the housing authority is not authorized to lend monies at an automatic loss—at a lower interest rate than the cost of funds—

the authority might have no choice but to call in the portion of the bond issue that is represented by the unappropriated funds.

Because of the possibility of an extraordinary call, municipal bond investors should exercise great caution in the purchase of housing bonds, especially at a price above that at which the bonds can be redeemed by the issuer. In the case of full coupon bonds, the securities most often can be called for extraordinary reasons at par (100 percent of face value). An extraordinary call at par is permitted even if the bond issuer can only refund the entire issue at a premium to par beginning at some future date.

Zero-coupon housing bonds generally can be called for extraordinary reasons at their accreted values (the current value on the books of the bond issuer) at any time, even if the normal call provision requires that the call price be at some premium of the accreted value, i.e., at 102 percent of the accreted value. The extraordinary call provision makes zero-coupon housing bonds even more difficult to evaluate than housing bonds with full coupons.

An investor who does not understand the call futures applicable to a particular bond can be easily "picked off" by an unscrupulous bond dealer or an uninformed broker who offers a housing bond at what seems to be a relatively high yield compared to the yields that are available on other tax-exempts. This high yield might soon evaporate, however, and be replaced by a large capital loss when the bond is called at a price below that paid by the investor. Losses caused by housing bonds being called at a price below the investor's purchase price are a special concern for the owners of zero-coupon bonds, because many investors do not understand the concept of original issue yield and the yield's relationship to the bond's accreted value. An example of accreted value is illustrated in Exhibit 2-6.

Industrial Development/Industrial Revenue Bonds

In an effort to attract industry, many municipalities have formed industrial development authorities (also called industrial revenue authorities) to facilitate tax-advantaged financing for the benefit of companies that relocate or open a production facility in the geographic area served by the authority. The debt securities issued by

Exhibit 2-6
Accreted Values of Zero-Coupon Housing Bonds: An Illustration

The 1984 bond issue of the California Housing Finance Agency in Exhibit 2-5 contained a little over $15 million of zero-coupon bonds that the Agency referred to as "capital appreciation bonds" in the official offering statement. Slightly less than $8 million of the capital appreciation bonds were sold at a price of $823 per $5,000 value at maturity in 2001 to provide investors with an annual tax-free yield of 11 percent. The remaining capital appreciation bonds matured in 2016 and were sold for $142 per $5,000 value to provide a tax-exempt yield of 11.5 percent. Thus, an investor who purchased $10,000 worth of the 2016 bonds at the time of issue could expect to recover $352,000 at maturity if the bonds were not called and were paid in full on the scheduled maturity date. The schedule for the accreted value of the 2001 bond (per $5,000 maturity value) was:

Date	Accreted Value	Date	Accreted Value	Date	Accreted Value
2/1/85	$ 854.18	2/1/91	$1,624.09	8/1/96	$2.926.97
8/1/85	901.17	8/1/91	1,713.43	2/1/97	3,087.97
2/1/86	950.74	2/1/92	1,807.68	8/1/97	3,257.83
8/1/86	1,003.03	8/1/92	1,907.12	2/1/98	3,487.03
2/1/87	1,058.21	2/1/93	2,012.02	8/1/98	3,626.09
8/1/87	1,116.41	8/1/93	2,122.69	2/1/99	3,626,09
2/1/88	1,177.82	2/1/94	2,289.46	8/1/99	4,035.98
8/1/88	1,242.61	8/1/94	2,362.64	2/1/00	4,257.99
2/1/89	1,383.08	2/1/95	2,492.60	8/1/00	4,492.21
8/1/89	1,383.08	8/1/95	2,629.71	2/1/01	4,739.31
2/1/90	1,539.42	2/1/96	2,774.36	8/1/01	5,000.00
8/1/90	1,539.42				

Exhibit 2-7
Industrial Development Bonds: An Illustration

In September 1989, the Development Authority of Columbus, Georgia, issued $1.75 million of revenue refunding bonds to redeem another series of bonds that had been issued at a higher rate of interest in 1984. Both the original 1984 issue and the 1989 refunding issue were used to finance three two-story office buildings that were leased to a private concern. Interest and principal on the bonds were payable only from revenues that the Authority derived from leasing or selling the project.

Because investors tend to be wary of bonds backed by an uncertain or unknown revenue source, the Development Authority obtained a letter of credit from Columbus Bank and Trust Company that guaranteed payment of principal and interest in case the lease payments were interrupted. The bonds in the issue were rated A+ and carried interest rates that ranged from 6.2 percent for those bonds maturing in one year to 7 percent for the longest bonds that matured twenty years following the year of issue.

---

the authorities are known as industrial development bonds (IDBs) or industrial revenue bonds (IRBs).

Municipalities are interested in promoting industrial development because of the economic growth and new jobs that will result. The municipality is not the only party that benefits from this type of financing, of course. A company that is being wooed by an industrial development group has the opportunity to obtain financing for its production facility at a substantially lower cost than the firm would have to pay if ordinary methods of financing were used.

Because the interest that investors receive from IDBs or IRBs usually will be exempt from federal, and in most instances state and local income taxes, companies are able to obtain financing at a substantially lower cost than if the firms were to finance the same facilities by borrowing from commercial banks or insurance companies or by issuing bonds via the corporate bond market. Regular sources of financing have a higher cost of funds because the interest income that lenders receive is subject to federal, state, and local income taxes. Thus, when using regular sources of financing, the lender must earn a higher interest rate to obtain the same after-tax return as that paid by industrial development bonds.

It is quite appropriate to compare the riskiness of an industrial development bond to that of a commercial loan or a corporate bond, because securities issued by an industrial development/revenue authority remain the credit responsibility of the company that utilizes the facilities; industrial development bonds are *not* obligations of the local municipality in whose name the industrial development/revenue authority is established.

Financing with tax-exempt bonds was becoming increasingly prevalent in the mid-1980s when Congress determined that many of the securities being issued under the auspices of industrial development/revenue authorities primarily were benefiting a select few within the community rather than the community as a whole. The issue of who was benefiting from industrial development bonds was a concern to both the federal government and to the municipalities that were issuing the bonds. The federal government was missing out on tax revenues because of the huge amount of tax-exempt interest being paid. For municipalities, the cost of issuing alternative types of municipal bonds was being forced higher than underlying economic conditions warranted, because significant sums of investor capital were being sucked up by the industrial development bonds. Thus, Joe and Laura Taxpayer were being forced to pay higher federal taxes because of a reduction in collections from a limited segment of the population (buyers of the IDBs), at the same time that there was pressure for higher state and local taxes to support the higher interest payments on state and county general obligation bonds that were competing in the market with industrial development bonds for investment funds.

The desire to control unwarranted and abusive financing with tax-exempt industrial development and industrial revenue bonds produced legislation that now separates bonds into two categories, *public purpose* and *private purpose,* depending upon the type of project an issue of securities is used to finance. The distinction between public purpose and private purpose bonds is discussed later in this chapter and in Appendix D. For now, suffice it to say that the interest from some IDBs and IRBs issued after August 8, 1986, is subject to the alternative minimum tax. The distinction between public purpose and private purpose municipal financing may or may not affect the tax liability of an individual who invests in IDBs or IRBs that are subject to the AMT. The change does affect the resale value of an AMT bond, however, because interest paid by the issuer will not be tax-exempt for all investors who might otherwise consider buying the security. Thus, it behooves investors to make certain that they are appropriately compensated up front, i.e., that they receive a higher yield when purchasing bonds subject to AMT than they do when purchasing bonds that are exempt from AMT.

Electric Utility Revenue Bonds

Some municipalities, including a range of governments from that of Lakeland, Florida, to the state of Nebraska, own all or part of their community's electrical generating or distribution facilities. In other communities, large stockholder-owned utility companies such as Southern California Edison and Louisiana Power & Light have an exclusive franchise to sell electricity. Still other regions are served by cooperatives that generate and/or distribute electricity to the public. In all three cases, organizations that produce and/or distribute electricity often utilize the municipal bond market to raise the funds that finance all or part of their facilities.

Stockholder-owned utilities that normally are required to borrow funds by issuing bonds that pay taxable interest may utilize an industrial revenue authority to tap the municipal bond market. Bonds issued through an industrial revenue authority generally are utilized to finance pollution control equipment. These bonds, called *pollution control revenue bonds,* are the fiscal responsibility of the respective electric utility company for whom the financing is being arranged. As in the case of the industrial development and industrial revenue bonds already discussed, repayment of electrical revenue bonds most definitely is *not* the responsibility of the municipality or the industrial revenue authority that permitted the local utility to issue bonds in the municipal bond market under the authority's name. Thus, electric utility revenue bonds should be

---

Exhibit 2-8
A Look at a Major Issuer of
Tax-Exempt Electric Utility Revenue Bonds

The Municipal Electric Authority of Georgia (MEAG) is a large issuer of tax-exempt bonds. The Authority was created by the state of Georgia to own and operate electric generation and transmission facilities that supply bulk electric power to political subdivisions—cities—in the state of Georgia. These cities then distribute the electricity and bill their own customers.

Payments to the holders of MEAG's securities are guaranteed by revenues that the Authority earns from selling electrical power to the cities. Although the Authority was created by the state of Georgia, the state does not stand behind the bonds and is not obligated to make any payments on the bonds. Thus, while the bonds of the state of Georgia command a rating of AAA, bonds of the Municipal Electric Authority of Georgia are given a rating a notch lower at AA.

---

judged by investors on the credit merit of the electric utility company or the cooperative for which the financing is being arranged.

The financial strength of an electric utility's balance sheet and the utility's capacity to cover interest charges on its bonds and to repay principal on its debt are influenced by many factors, including: 1) the political status of the public utility commissioners who must oversee electric rate increase requests (e.g., are the commissioners elected or appointed?); 2) the ever-changing demand for electricity as the population of the community being served wanes or grows or as electricity users change their consumption habits; 3) the electrical generating capacity of the company's power plants relative to its customers' peak demand for power; 4) the type of fuel used by the utility and the fuel's availability at a reasonable cost; 5) the concern for public safety, especially with regard to accidents in the instance of nuclear power plants and pollution in the instance of coal-fired power plants; and 6) the relative interest rates of existing debt and the maturity schedule and sinking fund requirements for the issuer's existing bonds.

Electric utilities incurred billions of dollars of debt over the past two decades as they significantly expanded their electrical generating and distribution capacities. The expansion occurred at the same time that the consuming public was reducing its demand for power or—depending on the area of the country—the rate at which the demand for energy was growing. Increased capacity, combined with higher electricity prices and a heightened environmental awareness, has resulted in many areas of the country being in a position in which they do not foresee the need for any additional major power plant expansions for some time to come.

Much of the financing that occurred in the late 1970s and early 1980s was at middle to high double-digit taxable interest rates and at lower double-digit tax-exempt interest rates. Many utilities have since refinanced this debt at a substantial reduction in interest costs. Combined with the fact that utilities have finally been able to bring newly constructed power plants into their rate bases and bill customers for these facilities, the electric utility industry is in substantially improved health in comparison to its condition several years ago.

TAXABLE MUNICIPAL BONDS

One of the more unusual investment products that evolved from the Tax Reform Act of 1986 is the taxable municipal bond. The Act established restrictions on the issuance of tax-exempt bonds that produced this new class of interest-bearing municipal bonds that pay interest investors must report as taxable income. This new classification of securities made the terms *municipal securities* and *tax-exempt* no longer synonymous, as least at the federal level.

Because taxable municipal securities make interest payments that investors must report as income for federal tax purposes, the bonds must provide investors with substantially higher yields than tax-exempt municipals of similar risk and maturity. For example, a taxable municipal with a fifteen-year maturity and an AA rating might yield 9.5 percent at the same time that a similar tax-exempt bond yields 7.8 percent. Because of the interest rate difference that exists between taxable and tax-exempt bonds, municipalities prefer to issue securities of the tax-exempt variety. However, the Tax Re-

---

Exhibit 2-9
An Illustration of a Taxable Municipal Bond Issue

In early 1987, the Massachusetts Municipal Wholesale Electric Company (MMWEC) issued taxable bonds with a thirty-year maturity that carried an 11.75 percent coupon. These BBB-rated bonds provided a substantially higher taxable yield than was available from similarly rated taxable bonds of investor-owned utilities. At the same time that this agency representing thirty-three Massachusetts municipal electric systems issued these taxable bonds, it also issued tax-exempt securities with an 8.75 percent coupon. Both bond issues were backed by power sales agreements with the agency's participants.

---

form Act set limits on the amounts of tax-exempt securities that can be issued and on the types of projects that can be financed (e.g., convention centers and sports stadiums are excluded) in this manner. The result is that municipalities sometimes decide to utilize more borrowed funds than are acceptable under restrictions of the Tax Reform Act.

By and large, taxable municipals have not been a particularly popular security for investors. It seems that investors who are interested in taxable fixed income securities opt either for U.S. treasuries (for safety) or corporates (for yield). Investors are attracted to municipal securities because of the tax-free income municipal bonds provide. If the exemption is removed, the majority of investors move on to another type of fixed income investment.

The general lack of interest in taxable municipals does not mean that these securities should be overlooked intentionally when you are putting together a portfolio of fixed income securities as a lack of investor demand may produce some attractive investment opportunities. For one thing, the majority of these securities are exempt from taxation by the respective states in which they are issued. For investors residing in states that impose a personal income tax, the exemption provides taxable municipal bonds with a relative advantage compared to corporate securities (but not Treasuries).

Taxable municipal bonds also benefit from a spillover effect from the impressive safety record of municipal bonds. Because of the outstanding record that municipalities have accumulated in honoring their obligations, taxable municipals tend to carry respectable ratings that make these securities desirable investments for conservative investors who do not mind owning a taxable security. As is the case with any municipal bond, however, the safety of a particular bond is dependent upon the facts that apply to that bond.

MATURITY AVAILABILITY

Investors interested in purchasing municipal bonds have a selection of securities with virtually any maturity lengths that their tax-shy hearts desire. If an A-rated municipal bond with a fifteen-year maturity is unavailable as part of a new issue on a particular day, a security with virtually identical characteristics is likely to be offered in the secondary market.

Maturities in the Secondary Market

Many bonds continue to trade in the secondary market for years or decades after their issue date, depending upon their original maturities and call features. At any point in time these bonds provide investors with securities that cover the whole spectrum of risk and maturities. A bond that was issued fifteen years ago with an original maturity of twenty-five years has a current maturity of ten years and trades in the secondary market like a ten-year bond (which, of course, it is). The number and variety of municipal bonds trading in the secondary market are virtually endless.

Of course, not all bonds issued in prior years will continue to trade until maturity. Many bonds will have been redeemed prior to maturity while other bonds may have been purchased by investors who intended to hold the securities until maturity. In addition, bonds from a particular issue may trade only occasionally rather than every day. Bonds are only available for purchase in the secondary market if an owner of the bonds offers the securities for sale.

Although the secondary market may not always offer the bonds of a specific maturity that were issued by a particular municipality, an investor (actually, the investor's broker) generally can locate a municipal issue with virtually identical maturity and risk character-istics to the desired bond. Thus, an investor might have to accept a twenty-year bond issued by Kansas City, Missouri, as a substitute for a virtually identical twenty-year bond issued by St. Louis, Mis-souri.

Maturities in the Primary Market

A wide range of bond maturities also is available in the primary market (i.e., the new issue market) for municipal securities. The range in maturities in the primary market stems both from the number of new issues that come to market and from the peculiar characteristics of individual municipal bond issues.

To retire debt in a timely and orderly fashion, a municipality frequently will establish the maturity schedule on a new bond issue so that a small portion of the issue comes due within one year, with additional bonds scheduled for maturity in succeeding years. Most

---

EXHIBIT 2-10
Maturity Schedule for an Issue of Housing Revenue Bonds

In late 1989, the Nevada Housing Division issued $44 million of single family program housing bonds that were backed by federally insured and guaranteed mortgage loans. The issue's serial senior bonds would mature in six-month intervals beginning on April 1, 1992, and continuing through October 1, 1999. The shortest bonds carried a tax-exempt yield of 6.3 percent and the October 1999 bonds would provide investors with a yield of 7 percent. Approxi-mately $250,000 face amount of the bonds matured every six months. The issue also had large amounts of term bonds that would mature in 2009, 2020, and 2021.

---

bond issues are structured so that increasing amounts of bonds come due in each succeeding year. These various maturities are referred to as serial maturities, and the bonds are known as serial bonds. Thus, a $50 million bond issue may have $100,000 of bonds coming due in the first year, $200,000 in the second year, $400,000 in the third year, $800,000 in the fourth year, $1 million in the fifth year, and so forth. After about twenty years, there might be a longer term issue that contains the bulk of the bond issue. There is likely to be a number of years between the maturity of the first term bond and the maturity of the last serial bond. For example, an issue may have serial bonds that mature annually for fifteen years and then two term bonds that mature in five years and ten years, respectively, after the last serial maturity.

While every bond issue is structured differently with respect to its maturity schedule, the cumulative effect of the trend among issues to skew maturity schedules on new bond issues toward the longer maturity range is that many more bonds are available for investors who will accept longer maturities. Some bond issues have term portions of the issues maturing as far out as forty years, although thirty years seems to be a more prevalent term for the longest portion of most municipal bond issues.

Many investors feel that bonds bought to be traded (as opposed to bonds acquired to produce interest income) are more tradable when the securities are part of the term portion of the issue. The difference in liquidity is caused by the term portion of the issue being more widely available so that traders become familiar with its specifics and, thus, feel more comfortable trading the bonds.

Investors who prefer shorter maturity periods for their bond investments have a few choices, although the availability of this type of security is limited. Some municipalities will issue notes in anticipation of taxes (these are called *tax anticipation notes* or *TANs*) or in anticipation of a longer term bond issue (these are called *bond anticipation notes* or *BANs*). These tax-exempt municipal securities generally come due within one year of the original issue date and frequently are purchased by institutional investors such as tax-exempt money market funds.

A recent phenomenon in the municipal bond market is the variable rate demand bond (VRDB). These bonds are also called *lower floaters* and *adjustable rate notes.* VRDBs usually are longer term issues that pay varying interest rates and that often provide investors with recurring put options (options to sell the bonds back to the issuer). For example, at a regular time interval the issuer can alter the interest rate that will be paid to the bondholder. At this same interval, the bondholder has the option to continue to hold the security at the new interest rate or to put the security to the issuer at some predetermined price, usually par. Variable rate demand bond issues frequently carry a letter of credit to assure investors that monies will be available in the event the bonds are put.

THE VARIETY OF MUNICIPAL SECURITIES: A SUMMARY

This chapter has focused on most of the major categories of municipal bonds available for purchase. There are taxable municipals, tax-exempt municipals, municipals with very short maturities, municipal bonds with very long maturities, and municipal bonds with maturities in between. Some municipal issues—actually, *most* municipal issues—are rated as very high quality while other municipal issues—generally municipal bonds of the revenue variety—sometimes carry lower ratings that indicate marginal credit safety.

An important lesson here is that all municipal bonds are not created equal. As is the case with corporate bonds, municipal securities have their little quirks. Thus, investors need to be informed before committing funds to the purchase of these securities.

_Chapter
Three_

THE RETURNS
FROM OWNING
MUNICIPAL BONDS

Although virtually every investor who purchases municipal bonds is concerned primarily with tax-free interest payments, there are other considerations when evaluating the returns from owning these securities. Municipal bonds are not always purchased at face value nor are they always held until maturity or sold at face value in the secondary market. Because municipal bonds are not always sold or redeemed at the same price at which they were purchased, expected changes in market value should be a consideration for investors when they evaluate potential returns.

The returns from municipal bonds essentially are identical in type, if not necessarily in size, to the returns from any type of investment asset. The investor's return consists of current income received during the holding period adjusted by any appreciation or depreciation in market value that may occur during the time the asset is owned. The convention is to calculate rates of return on an annualized basis so that the profitability of various investments can be compared.

The return from investments in common stocks is comprised of dividend payments (generally paid quarterly) and changes in market value. For bond investments, income consists of semi-annual interest payments in addition to any appreciation or depreciation in market value that occurs following the date of purchase.

RATES OF RETURN THAT ARE RELEVANT TO MUNICIPAL BONDS

There are several useful measures of return that are applicable to municipal bonds. To make each of the measures comparable with the returns from taxable securities, taxable yields must be adjusted for taxes paid on the income that is received. The adjustment, which is dependent upon the tax rate applicable to an individual investor, will be taken up later in this chapter. This section will concentrate on how different rates of return are calculated for tax-free municipal bonds.

Current Yield

Current yield, the most elementary yardstick of the return from a municipal bond, includes only annual interest payments. Thus, the current yield calculation excludes any expected or potential change in a municipal bond's market price.

The current yield of a municipal bond is calculated by dividing the annual interest (the sum of the two semi-annual interest payments) by the current market price of the bond. The formula for calculating this is:

$$\text{Current Yield} = \frac{\text{Annual Interest}}{\text{Market Value of Bond}} \qquad \text{(Equation 3-1)}$$

For example, a municipal bond with a 9 percent coupon rate (an annual interest payment equal to 9 percent of the $5,000 principal, or $450) and a current market price of 90 (90 percent of the $5,000 principal amount, or $4,500) provides an investor with a current yield of $450/$4,500 or 10 percent.

The current yield measure is incomplete and has inherent limitations for gauging an investor's return from owning a municipal bond because it does not take into account potential changes in market value. At the same time, however, current yield also has

---

Exhibit 3-1
Calculating a Municipal Bond's Current Yield

A $5,000 principal amount municipal bond issued in 1985 by the town of Greensburg, Indiana, is currently quoted at a price of 95 1/2 (e.g., 95.5 percent of the bond's principal). If the bond has a coupon rate of 8 percent, annual interest will equal 8 percent of $5,000, or $400. The Greensburg bond's current yield is calculated as:

$$\frac{\text{Annual Interest}}{\text{Market Value of Bond}} = \frac{\$400}{\$6,775} = 8.41\%$$

---

some advantages in comparison with other measures of return. For one thing, current yield is simple to compute and easy to understand. It makes no assumptions other than that interest payments will continue at the specified level so that there is no room for the errors that creep into calculations based on assumptions as to changes in market value. For individuals who are primarily interested in the income that is provided by a bond's interest payments, current yield can be a useful and important measure of a bond's return.

If a municipal bond sells at a discount from face value, current yield must be above the bond's stated coupon rate. In the previous example of the $5,000 principal bond selling at a $500 discount from its principal value, or $4,500, the coupon rate is 9 percent while the current yield is 10 percent.

A municipal bond that sells in the secondary market at a price that is greater than its par value has a current yield that is less than the stated coupon rate. For example, if the 9 percent coupon bond is quoted in the secondary market at 120 (120 percent of $5,000, or $6,000), the coupon rate and annual interest payment remain at 9 percent and $450, respectively. However, the current yield at the higher price is $450/$6,000, or 7.5 percent.

Investors must be cautious when utilizing current yield to evaluate a municipal bond. A bond with a high coupon relative to the coupons that are available on issues that are being sold at par in the primary market will sell at a premium to par value, but the high-coupon bond will still provide a very attractive current yield. In fact, the unusually high current yields that accompany premium bonds make the bonds appear to be much better investments than they actually are.

Suppose a 14 percent coupon municipal bond issued some years ago has 10 years remaining to maturity and the market rate of interest on new 10-year maturity issues of similar risk is 9 percent. Thus, a new 9 percent coupon bond with 10 years to maturity will sell at par. In a 9 percent interest environment, the 14 percent coupon bond should sell at a price of approximately 132, or $6,600. (The method for obtaining this price will be illustrated shortly.) At a price of $6,600 the bond's current yield is $700/$6,600, or 10.6 percent, a return that is substantially higher than the current yield of 9 percent on bonds that are being issued at par in the primary market. Is this unusually high current return really an accurate measure of the bond's return? In truth, the high current yield presents the bond in such a favorable light because this measure does not take into account the $320 loss in market value that must occur over the next 10 years as the bond moves toward maturity.

Thus, comparing a municipal bond's annual interest payments with the bond's market price produces a measure of yield that must be used with great care. Current yield can be an especially misleading measure of a bond's return when the maturity is short and the coupon is substantially different from the current market rate of interest. Only when the bond is selling at par and the investor is expecting to hold the security to maturity will the current yield tell the whole story. In other instances, such as when the municipal bond is bought at either a discount or a premium to face value, or when the bond may have to be sold prior to maturity at a price that is different from its purchase price, changes in market value are an important consideration in determining a municipal bond's total return.

Yield to Maturity

The most common measure of the return on municipal bond investments (or on any bond) is yield to maturity (YTM). Yield to matu-

---

Exhibit 3-2
Calculating the Current Yield for a Premium Bond

A \$5,000 principal amount, 15 percent coupon bond that was issued by the City of Valdosta, Georgia, during 1982 when market rates of interest reached historic highs is currently priced at 120 (a market value of 120 percent of \$5000, or \$6000). The Valdosta bond's current yield is calculated as:

$$\frac{\text{Annual Interest}}{\text{Market Value of Bond}} = \frac{\$750}{\$6,000} = 12.5\%$$

---

rity takes into account the annual interest payments and changes in the bond's market value that will occur between the date the calculation is made and the date the bond matures. If a bond has a market value of less than its principal amount (e.g., the bond sells at a discount), yield to maturity includes the price appreciation that must occur during the remaining time before the bond will be redeemed at face value. For a bond that sells above its face value (e.g., sells at a premium), yield to maturity includes the decline in value that must occur during the time until the bond matures at face value.

In technical terms, yield to maturity is the rate that equates the present value of an investor's cash outflows (the current market price that must be paid to acquire the bond) with the present value of the bond's cash payments (the semi-annual interest payments and the repayment of principal at maturity). In the following formula, i is the rate of discount (e.g., the yield to maturity) that equates the two cash streams:

$$M = \frac{I_1}{(1+i/2)^1} + \frac{I_2}{(1+i/2)^2} + \frac{I_3}{(1+i/2)^3} + \cdots\cdots \qquad \text{(Equation 3–2)}$$

$$+ \frac{I_n}{(1+i/2)^n} + \frac{P_n}{(1+i/2)^n}$$

where:

M = the market price of the bond

I = semi-annual interest payments on the bond

P   =   the principal to be repaid at maturity
n   =   the number of semi-annual interest payment periods
        until maturity
i   =   the yield to maturity

In Equation 3-2, n is the total number of interest payments over the life of the bond. Because municipal bonds make semi-annual interest payments, the number of payments equals twice the number of years until maturity. For example, eight interest payments will be made (e.g., n equals eight) if a bond has four years remaining until maturity.

There is one slight wrinkle in the calculation for a municipal bond's yield to maturity. Although interest payments on municipal bonds are generally free of taxation, any realized gain in market value at maturity (or when a bond is sold or redeemed prior to maturity) becomes taxable income to the investor. Thus, the yield to maturity for a municipal bond selling at a discount to its face value does not represent a return that is totally tax-free.

Although the yield to maturity for municipal bonds purchased at a discount must be adjusted downward somewhat when calculating the true after-tax yield, no equivalent adjustment is required when municipal bonds are purchased at a premium to their face values. The reason is that, for municipal bond investments, the premium paid above par value cannot be utilized to record a loss for tax purposes when the bonds mature. Thus, the yield to maturity is the true after-tax yield.

Equation 3-2 can be revised to calculate the tax-free return for a municipal bond that sells at a discount. Merely substitute the amount of cash that will be received after subtracting any resulting tax obligation (e.g., principal less the tax obligation) for the principal value of the bond as the final cash flow. Thus, if a $5,000 principal amount municipal bond with a 9 percent coupon and a three-year maturity is purchased for $4,700 (a price of 94), the $300 gain will be taxable at the taxpayer's marginal tax rate. For someone paying taxes at a rate of 25 percent, a tax of $75 (25 percent of the $300 gain) will result in the bondholder keeping $4,925 ($5,000 - $75) of the $5,000 principal. Exhibit 3-4 shows how the reduction in

---

Exhibit 3-3
The Calculation of Yield to Maturity

A \$5,000 principal amount municipal bond sells in the secondary market at a price of 91 (a market value of 91 percent of \$5,000, or \$4,500). If the bond matures in four years and has an 8 percent coupon rate, how is the equation to calculate yield to maturity set up if interest payments are made semi-annually?

$$\$910 = \frac{\$200}{(1+i/2)^1} + \frac{\$200}{(1+i/2)^2} + \cdots + \frac{\$200}{(1+i/2)^8} + \frac{\$5,000}{(1+i/2)^8}$$

where \$200 is the semi-annual interest payment (half the \$400 in annual interest) and i is the yield to maturity.

If interest is assumed to be paid annually rather than semi-annually, the calculation for yield to maturity is:

$$\$910 = \frac{\$400}{(1+i)^1} + \frac{\$400}{(1+i)^2} + \frac{\$400}{(1+i)^3} + \frac{\$400}{(1+i)^4} + \frac{\$5,000}{(1+i)^4}$$

---

an investor's cash flow because of the tax liability is taken into account in calculating the yield on this bond.

Suffice it to say that solving Equation 3-2 for yield to maturity requires a calculator or computer. Some of the more sophisticated small personal calculators will compute a bond's yield to maturity when the user inputs the security's market price, the size and number of interest payments, and the principal to be repaid at maturity.

Equation 3-3 frequently is employed to estimate a bond's yield to maturity. Although this alternate calculation produces only an approximate answer, the equation is much easier to work with than is Equation 3-2.

$$\text{YTM(approximate)} = \frac{I + (P - M)/n}{(M + P)/2} \qquad \text{(Equation 3-3)}$$

where:

I = annual interest payments (in dollars)

n = the number of years until the bond matures

Exhibit 3-4
Adjusting a Bond's Yield for Taxation of a Capital Gain

$$\text{Market Price} = \frac{I_1}{(1+i)^1} + \frac{I_3}{(1+i)^2} + \frac{I_3}{(1+i)^3} + \frac{\text{Principal} - \text{Tax}}{(1+i)^3}$$

$$\$4{,}700 = \frac{\$450}{(1+i)^1} + \frac{\$450}{(1+i)^2} + \frac{\$450}{(1+i)^3} + \frac{\$5{,}000 - \$75}{(1+i)^3}$$

$$\$4{,}700 = \frac{\$450}{(1+i)^1} = \frac{\$450}{(1+i)^2} + \frac{\$450}{(1+i)^3} + \frac{\$4{,}925}{(1+i)^3}$$

Where i is the investor's after-tax yield to maturity after adjusting for a 25 percent tax on the $300 gain that occurs because the bond is purchased at a $300 discount from face value.

M = the bond's current market price
p = the principal amount that will be paid at maturity

The top portion of Equation 3-3 sums the average annual increase or decrease in the bond's market value (the principal to be received at maturity less the market price) and the annual interest income (I) to obtain the average annual income that will be received by the bondholder. The bottom portion of Equation 3-3 calculates the average price at which the bond will sell during its remaining life. The average price is assumed to be the midpoint between the current price and the maturity value.

In the prior example of the 14 percent coupon bond with ten years of interest payments remaining until maturity and a market price of $6,000, Equation 3-3 calculates the yield to maturity as:

$$\text{YTM} = \frac{\$700 + (-\$1{,}600/10)}{(\$6{,}600 + \$5{,}000)/2} = \frac{\$540}{\$5{,}800} = 9.3\%$$

This equation gives a YTM measure of 9.3 percent that resembles closely the more accurate yield to maturity of almost exactly 9 percent calculated with Equation 3-2. However, even though Equation 3-3 results in an answer that is reasonably close to the true YTM, even relatively small yield differences are important when evaluating municipal bonds.

The yield to maturity of approximately 9 percent illustrates how current yield can be misleading as a measure of a municipal bond's return. In this case, the yield to maturity of 9 percent compares to a current yield of 10.6 percent. Purchasing this municipal bond solely on the basis of the current yield completely disregards the reduction in the bond's market value that must occur over the next ten years.

Differences between current yield and yield to maturity tend to be greatest when municipal bonds have short maturities. The ten-year bond in the previous example demonstrates this exaggerated difference. Differences between the two measures will be reduced when bonds have maturities of twenty to thirty years.

Yield to Call

The call feature that is part of many municipal bond issues was discussed briefly in Chapter 1. Basically, a call forces bondholders to sell bonds back to the issuer prior to maturity. Calls nearly always occur when market rates of interest have declined subsequent to the date of issue so that market rates of interest are below the coupon rate on the bonds. Thus, it is to the issuer's advantage to retire the bonds at the earliest possible date (the call date) rather than continue to pay interest on the bonds until their maturity. Funds to pay for the early retirement frequently are obtained by selling another issue of bonds at the reduced market rate of interest.

From an investor's perspective, the important aspect of owning a bond that is subject to being called is that the call date, not the maturity date, frequently dictates the life of the security. In general, a bond with a coupon rate that is significantly above the current market rate of interest is likely to be called. When a municipal bond sells at a significant premium to face value, an investor must question the broker about the terms of the bond with respect to the possibility of an early call.

Exhibit 3-5
Approximating a Municipal Bond's Yield to Maturity

A $5,000 principal, 6 percent coupon municipal bond issued by the City of New York in 1974 with a 30-year maturity currently sells in the secondary market at a price of 86. If the current year is 1992, the approximate yield to maturity using Equation 3-3 is:

$$YTM = \frac{\$300 + (\$5,000 - \$4,300)/12}{(\$4,300 + \$5,000)/2}$$

$$= \frac{\$300 + \$700/12}{\$9,300/2} = \frac{\$358}{\$4,650} = 7.7\%$$

The current yield for this bond is:

$$\frac{Annual\ Interest}{Market\ Price} = \frac{\$300}{\$4,300} = 7\%$$

Remember that this bond's 7.7 percent yield to maturity is not entirely tax-free because the investor will be required to declare the $700 gain as income during the year the bond matures (assuming the bond is held that long). For an investor in the 28 percent tax bracket, the after-tax gain on the bond would be reduced to $504 ($700 less 28 percent of $700), and the yield to maturity would fall from 7.7 percent to 7.35 percent. Thus, the investor would earn an after-tax return of approximately 7.35 percent.

In calculating the return on a municipal bond that is likely to be called, the investor should substitute the call date for the maturity date and the price at which the bond will be called for the principal repayment. Most call features stipulate a call price that is at a premium to par with the premium gradually declining to zero (e.g., the call price declining to par) over the life of the bond. If the bond is callable at par, as are many public housing issues or bonds near maturity, the terminal value of the bond on the call date will be the same as the bond's principal. Equation 3-4 illustrates the slight modification to Equation 3-3 that produces the yield to call.

$$YTC = \frac{I + (P_c - M)/c}{(M + P_c)/2}$$

(Equation 3-4)

where:

YTC = the yield to call
I = the annual interest payment
c = the number of years until the bond will be called
M = the current market price of the bond
P_c = the call price

As an illustration, suppose a 14 percent coupon, $5,000 principal amount bond with ten years remaining until maturity contains a call feature that permits the issuer to redeem the bond at a price of 105 (a premium of 5 percent above the face value, or $5,250) beginning five years prior to the scheduled maturity. Because there is such a great difference between the current 9 percent market rate of interest and the 14 percent coupon rate on the bond, it is virtually certain that the issuer will call the bonds on the earliest possible date. Assuming a current price of $6,600, the yield to call is estimated by substituting the $5,250 call price for the $5,000 principal and reducing the maturity length from ten to five years. The result is illustrated in Exhibit 3-6.

The bond's low yield to call is caused by the expected $1,350 capital loss that will occur in the relatively short five-year period between the purchase date and the call date. The average annual loss of $270 ($1,350/5 years) offsets a substantial portion of each $700 annual interest payment and produces a relatively low yield to call. In fact, this bond will sell in the secondary market at a price that produces a yield to call that is essentially the same as the yields that are available on other five-year investments of comparable risk.

It is unlikely that issuers will call bonds that sell at a discount from their call prices (it would be less expensive for the issuer to purchase the bonds in the open market) so that yield to maturity rather than yield to call should be used when evaluating discount bonds. There is always the possibility that interest rates will fall, however, so that a bond's call price can seldom be altogether ignored. The call price on discount bonds may act to keep the bonds from having much upside potential in market price if interest rates

---

Exhibit 3-6
Calculating a Municipal Bond's Yield to Call

A $5,000 principal amount, 14 percent coupon bond is offered in the secondary market at a price of 132 (132 percent of the bond's $5,000 principal, or $6,600). The bond has a ten-year maturity but can be called by the issuer at the call price of 105 beginning five years prior to maturity. The approximate yield to call is calculated using Equation 3-4 as follows:

$$YTM = \frac{\$300 + (\$5,000 - \$4,300)/12}{(\$4,300 + \$5,000)/2}$$

$$= \frac{\$300 + \$700/12}{\$9,300/2} = \frac{\$358}{\$4,650} = 7.7\%$$

---

should fall, because investors know that the bonds may be lost prior to maturity through a call by the issuer.

Yield to Put

Yield to put is a measure of return that rarely is used simply because most municipal bonds are not subject to being put back to the issuer. A put feature permits a bondholder to force the issuer to repurchase the bond at a designated price, generally face value, on a specified date or on a series of dates prior to the scheduled maturity. Essentially, a put permits an investor to back out early from an agreement that is normally binding (to the investor) through the maturity date. Just as an issuer is not required to exercise the right to call a bond issue, a bondholder does not have to exercise the right to force the issuer to repurchase the bond prior to maturity. A call is at the option of the issuer but a put is at the option of the bondholder.

A municipal bond with a put feature will be put to the issuer when market rates of interest have risen above the bond's coupon rate. The put allows the bondholder to cut the contract short (e.g., have the principal returned prior to maturity) so that funds returned by the issuer can be reinvested at the higher market rate of interest. If market rates of interest have fallen since the issue date, the bond will sell at a premium, and if the put feature stipulates a put at par, the option will not be utilized by the bondholder. It is not to an investor's advantage to sell a bond to the issuer at par when the security can be sold at a premium in the secondary market.

Yield to put is calculated by making slight alterations to either Equation 3-2 or Equation 3-3. Simply replace the number of years until maturity with the number of years to the date the bond can be put and substitute the price at which the bond can be put for the par value to be returned at maturity. If the price of the put is the same as the par value, there will be no change in the top portion of the equation. The equation for computing yield to put is:

$$YTP = \frac{I + (P_p - M)/p}{(M + P_p)/2}$$

(Equation 3-5)

where:

YTP = the yield to put
I = the annual interest payment
P_p = the price at which the bond can be put to the issuer
p = the number of years until the put can occur
M = the current market price of the bond

Suppose the ten-year municipal bond outlined in the preceding example has a 6 percent coupon rather than the 14 percent coupon previously assumed. Interest payments each year will amount to $300 ($5,000 x .06), and the bond should sell in the secondary market at a price of approximately $4,035 if the market rate of interest is 9 percent. (This market price is calculated using either Equation 3-2 or Equation 3-3.)

Now assume that the same bond in an identical interest rate environment has a put feature that permits the bondholder to sell the bond at par back to the issuer five years prior to maturity. Thus, the ten-year bond has an expected life of only five years. The yield to put is calculated with Equation 3-5 and compared with the yield to maturity in Exhibit 3-7.

Because the bondholder can either force the issuer to repurchase the bond at the end of five years or allow the bond to remain outstanding to ten years, the higher of either the yield to put or the yield to maturity is the relevant measure of return in evaluating any bond with a put option. In this example, the yield to put is higher than the yield to maturity, so the bond's yield to put should be the measure of return that influences the investor's decision about whether to purchase or continue to hold the municipal bond.

When comparing yield to maturity and yield to call, the lower of the two rates is the applicable measure because with a call feature the bond issuer, not the investor, is able to decide when the bond will be retired. The issuer will attempt to minimize the cost of funds, which, in turn, minimizes the investor's rate of return.

TAXES AND RATES OF RETURN

Making informed investment decisions requires that an individual understand how taxes will affect an asset's return. Taxes are an evil to be avoided or, at least, minimized (but not evaded!) unless the cost of avoidance is too high. That is, the returns that are available from tax-advantaged investments (including, of course, municipal bonds) may be so low relative to the returns on fully taxable investments that many investors are better off acquiring taxable investments and paying the required assessment. It is worthwhile to spend some time reviewing income taxes and their effect on investment decisions.

Making Decisions at the Margin

Economics professors have long (and generally not successfully) taught that economic decisions should be made at the margin. Managers must look at the extra expense—called the *marginal cost*—not at the total cost or average cost when making expansion and input decisions. A firm's executives must examine additional revenues—termed *marginal revenues*—not just the prices or the level of total revenues when making pricing and output decisions.

The logic for businesses to use marginal decision-making also applies to individual investors—that is, investors should evaluate

---

Exhibit 3-7
Calculating the Yield to Put for a Municipal Bond

Assume that a $5,000 principal, 6 percent coupon municipal bond with a ten-year maturity is trading in the secondary market at a price of $4,035. The bond has a put feature that permits the owner to sell the bond to the issuer at par five years prior to the scheduled maturity. With Equation 3-5, the approximate yield to put is calculated as:

$$YTP = \frac{I + (P_p - M)/p}{(M + P_p)/2}$$

$$= \frac{(\$300 + (\$5,000 - \$4,035)/5}{(\$4,035 + \$5,000)/2}$$

$$= \frac{\$300 + \$965/5}{\$9,035/2} = \frac{\$493}{\$4,517.50} = 10.9\%$$

The bond's yield to maturity is calculated as:

$$YTM = \frac{(\$300 + (\$5,000 - \$4,035)/10}{\$4,035 + \$5,000)/2}$$

$$= \frac{\$300 + \$965/10}{\$9,035/2} + \frac{\$396.50}{\$4,517.50} = 8.8\%$$

---

marginal returns when making investment decisions. Marginal returns are the returns that remain after any expenses, including applicable taxes, are deducted. The taxes that will have to be paid (or that can be saved) on extra income are an expense that must be considered by individual investors.

Marginal Tax Rates

Many individuals mistakenly believe that the rates of taxation applicable to different income levels applies not just to income within the respective brackets but, rather, to all income. In other words, they believe that an individual who receives a wage increase and thereby moves into a higher tax bracket will be required to pay the higher tax rate on all income, including income that formerly was taxed at a lower rate. This view of taxation is incorrect.

Nearly all income taxes, including the federal income tax and most state and local income taxes, are constructed so that different rates apply to income that falls within specific brackets. A tax with progressively higher rates that are applied to higher levels of income is termed a *progressive* tax. In the United States, moving into a higher tax bracket as a result of receiving additional income results in a higher tax rate only on the additional income, and perhaps not on all of that. Tax brackets define the income tax rates that individuals must pay on additions to income, not on total income.

An example of a progressive tax is a 10 percent levy on all income up to $10,000, a 15 percent tax on all income *from* $10,000 to $20,000, and a 25 percent tax on all income *over* $20,000. Each of the three rates applies only to the income that is included in that rate's respective bracket, not to total income. Utilizing these hypothetical brackets, an individual with a taxable income of $22,000 will pay a tax of:

$$(\$10,000)(.10) + (\$10,000)(.15) + (\$2,000)(.25) = \$3,000$$

It is the rate on additional income that must be paid in taxes, frequently called the *marginal* tax rate, that should be employed in making investment decisions. The average tax rate, e.g., the percentage of total income that must be paid in taxes, is interesting to know but is of little consequence in decision-making. For example, if an individual earns $50,000 and pays $12,000 in income taxes, the average tax rate is 24 percent ($12,000/$50,000). However, this rate provides no guidance for making important investment decisions such as how much in taxes will be saved if the investor is able to hide some existing income from taxation.

Understanding marginal tax rates is critical for any investor who wishes to compare investment alternatives on the basis of after-tax return. After-tax return can be calculated only by using an individual's marginal tax rate. Suppose an investor must choose between an asset that pays a fully taxable return of 12 percent and a second asset that pays a tax-free return of 6 percent. If the individual is in the 25 percent marginal tax bracket, the after-tax return on the taxable asset is 9 percent (12 percent minus 0.25 of 12 percent), a level that is significantly higher than the 6 percent return from the tax-free asset. Only when the individual's marginal tax rate exceeds 50 percent will this tax-free investment produce a higher after-tax return than the return provided by the taxable investment. The higher an individual's marginal tax rate, the more likely that a tax-free investment will provide an after-tax return that is superior to the returns provided by taxable investments.

The Value of the Federal Income Tax Exemption

The benefit of owning a municipal bond is a direct function of the investor's marginal federal income tax rate. The marginal tax rates illustrated in Exhibit 3-10 were in effect in 1991. Americans face a progressive federal income tax in which there are three separate rates applicable to three ranges of income.

The last section examined a method of comparing taxable and tax-free returns, an exercise of particular importance to investors who are considering the acquisition of municipal bonds. To compare the returns from municipal bonds with returns on taxable investments, it is necessary to convert a tax-free return to a taxable return, or vice-versa. The conversion is influenced by the investor's

---

Exhibit 3-8
Calculating the After-Tax Cost of a Tax Deductible Expense

Assume that John Mull has a sufficient amount of deductions that for tax purposes he is able to itemize various investment expenses and is now considering whether to subscribe to an investment advisory letter that costs $400 per year. The expense of the letter is deductible, and John pays taxes at a marginal rate of 28 percent of income. What will be the after-tax cost of the subscription?

$$\text{After–Tax Cost} = \text{Cost} - \text{Tax Savings}$$
$$= \$400 - (\$400)\,(.28)$$
$$= \$400 - \$112$$
$$= \$288$$

---

marginal income tax rate so that a first step is to examine Exhibit 3-10 and determine the appropriate federal income tax rate.

Equation 3-6 is used to determine the taxable return that is equivalent to a given tax-free return. The conversion of a tax-free return to a taxable return permits an investor to determine whether the returns on taxable investments such as corporate bonds, certificates of deposit, and preferred stocks are competitive with the tax-exempt return that can be earned on a municipal bond.

Exhibit 3-9
Comparing Taxable and Tax-Free Returns

Richard Beuther's ace broker, Bill Toyne, calls about some bonds that have just become available. Richard has a choice of a $5,000 principal amount municipal bond that yields a tax-exempt return of 7 percent, or a $5,000 principal amount corporate bond that yields a taxable annual return of 11 percent. Both bonds sell at par, have identical maturities, and are similar in risk. Thus, only the value of the tax exemption on the municipal bond is a consideration in the selection. If Richard pays taxes at a marginal rate of 28 percent, which alternative should be elected?

For the corporate bond:

$$
\begin{aligned}
\text{After--Tax Profit} &= \text{Interest Income} - \text{Taxes} \\
&= (.11 \times \$5,000) - (.11 \times \$5,000)(.28) \\
&= \$555 - \$155.40 \\
&= \$399.60
\end{aligned}
$$

$$
\begin{aligned}
\text{After--Tax Return} &= \text{After--Tax Profit} / \text{Amount Invested} \\
&= \$399.60 / \$5,000 \\
&= 8.0\%
\end{aligned}
$$

Because this after-tax return on the taxable corporate bond is greater than the 7 percent return on the tax-free municipal, Richard should select the corporate bond.

(Equation 3-6)

$$EquivalentTaxableYield \ = \ \frac{Tax\ Free\ Yield}{1 - Marginal\ Tax\ Rate}$$

Assume that a single individual with a taxable income of $50,000 has the opportunity to purchase at face value an 8 percent coupon municipal bond. To calculate the taxable return that will make the municipal bond and a taxable investment of equivalent risk and maturity equal, insert the appropriate marginal tax rate from Exhibit 3-10 into Equation 3-6 and obtain .08/(1 - .31) = .08/.69 = .116, or 11.6 percent. Thus, for an investor in the 31 percent federal tax bracket, a taxable return of 11.6 percent and the municipal bond's tax-free return of 8 percent offer the same returns.

The first two columns of Exhibit 3-12 illustrate the dollar amounts for this example. The third column of Exhibit 3-12 calculates the after-tax income from the same 12 percent bond that is applicable to an investor who pays federal income taxes at a marginal rate of 28 percent. For an investor in the 28 percent marginal tax bracket, the after-tax income from the taxable 12 percent coupon bond is higher than the after-tax income from the 8 percent municipal bond so that the investor should select the taxable bond. This example illustrates why an investor in a low tax bracket may be better served by selecting taxable investments. Again, the lower an investor's effective tax rate, the less likely that municipal bonds (or any tax-advantaged investments) are fitting investment vehicles.

Exhibit 3-10
Taxable Income and Marginal Federal Tax Rates for 1991

	Taxable Income	
Marginal Tax Rate	Individual Returns	Joint Returns
15%	$ 0 to $19,450	$ 0 to $ 32,450
28	19,451 to 47,050	32,451 to 78,400
31	all over 47,050	all over 78,400

Exhibit 3-11
Calculating an Investor's Federal Tax Liability

Steve Wilkinson, an important executive with a large national communications company, had a taxable income of $56,000 last year. Using the column in Exhibit 3-10 that is applicable to individual investors, Steve's federal income tax liability is calculated as:

Taxable Income			Tax	
15% of the first	$19,450.00			$ 2,917.50
28% of the next	27,600.00			7,728.00
31% of the next	8,950.00			2,774.50
Total Income	$56,000.00		Tax	$13,420.00

Steve is in the 31 percent marginal tax bracket even though the average tax rate paid is $13,420.00/$56,000, or 24 percent.

Equation 3-6 can be rearranged slightly to provide guidance on the after-tax rate that is required to make an investor indifferent to a given taxable yield. Multiplying both sides of Equation 3-6 by (1 - marginal tax rate) results in:

(Equation 3-7)

Equivalent Tax-Free Yield =
Taxable Yield × (1 − Marginal Tax Rate)

If a single investor has a taxable income of $35,000 and a marginal tax rate of 28 percent (from Exhibit 3-10), the yield from a tax-free investment must be at least 8.64 percent [.12(1 - .28) = .0864] to provide a return that is equivalent to the taxable yield of 12 percent. Thus, if a 12 percent taxable bond is available at the same time as an 8 percent tax-free municipal bond, an investor in the 28 percent tax bracket should select the taxable alternative because the taxable bond provides a greater after-tax income (third column of Exhibit 3-12).

The Value of the State Income Tax Exemption

For investors residing in states that do not have a state income tax or in states that do not exempt any municipal bond interest from state income taxation, there is no additional income tax benefit to the federal tax exemption from municipal bond interest. For investors residing in states that do exempt municipal bond interest, an added tax advantage exists for investors who own municipal bonds that qualify for the exemption.

For residents of states with an income tax that exempts municipal bond interest, the value of the exemption depends upon two factors: the marginal rate of income taxation applied by the state and whether the investor utilizes state income tax payments as an itemized deduction in calculating the federal tax liability. A higher marginal state tax rate and an inability to use the state tax to reduce federal taxes increases the value of the state tax exemption of municipal bond interest.

Suppose an individual does not itemize deductions for federal tax purposes because total itemized deductions do not exceed the standard deduction that a taxpayer is permitted to claim. In this case, the taxable equivalent yield calculation of Equation 3-6 is altered slightly and becomes:

$$\text{Taxable Equivalent Yield} = \frac{\text{Nontaxable Yield}}{(1 - t_f - t_s)} \qquad \text{(Equation 3-8)}$$

Exhibit 3-12
Comparing Taxable and Nontaxable Investment Alternatives

	8 % Municipal Bond (31% tax rate)	12% Taxable Bond (31% tax rate)	12% Taxable Bond (28% tax rate)
Annual Income from Bond*	$800	$1,200	$1,200
Tax	0	372	336
After-Tax Income	$800	$ 828	$ 864

* Assumes a $10,000 investment in each bond

---

where:

t_f =   the marginal rate of federal taxation
t_s =   the marginal rate of state taxation

To understand how federal and state income taxes work in combination to affect the decision of whether to purchase municipals or taxable securities, suppose a married investor has a taxable income of \$90,000, resulting in a marginal federal income tax rate of 33 percent. Now assume the individual lives in a state that taxes all income at a flat rate of 6 percent and that the investor does not deduct state income tax payments for computing federal taxes. If the investor locates a municipal bond with a tax-free yield of 8.0 percent (tax-free at both the federal and state levels), Equation 3-8 computes the taxable yield required to provide the same after-tax return:

$$\frac{.08}{(1 - .31 - .06)} = \frac{.08}{(1 - .37)} = \frac{.08}{.63} = .127, \text{ or } 12.7\%$$

Thus, the investor requires a 12.7 percent yield on a taxable security to earn the same return as a municipal bond that provides an 8 percent return. Now suppose the same investor locates a taxable bond yielding 10.7 percent and wishes to determine the yield on a tax-free municipal that will provide the same after-tax return. Rearranging Equation 3-8 produces:

Tax-Free Yield = Taxable Yield $\times$ $(1 - t_f - t_s)$ (Equation 3-9)

To match the taxable bond yielding 10.7 percent, a tax-free bond must yield .107 x (1–.31–.06) which equals .65, or 6.5 percent.

If an investor resides in a state without a state income tax or in a state that does not exempt interest on municipal bonds from taxation, t_s in Equations 3-0 and 3-9 will equal zero. In the example just discussed, if the investor lives in a state that taxes municipal interest or a state that levies no income tax, the yield on a municipal bond required to match the taxable return of 10.7 percent will be .107 x (1-.31) which equals .074, or 7.4 percent. The higher required return on tax-free municipals results from the lack of additional tax savings at the state level.

Now suppose that the investor itemizes deductions at the federal level. Because payments of state income taxes (but not state sales

---

Exhibit 3-13
Choosing Between Taxable and Nontaxable Yields

Kent Moore's broker, I. Gotem Now, calls with news of a planned General Motors bond issue that will carry a yield of 10.75 percent. Knowing that GM bonds pay taxable interest, Kent asks the broker for the current yield on a comparable municipal bond. The broker responds that nontaxable bonds of similar maturity and risk are yielding 7.3 percent. Kent, who is in the 28 percent marginal income tax bracket, must decide between the two alternatives.

Using Equation 3-7, Kent can calculate the equivalent tax-free yield required to match the taxable General Motors bond:

$$
\begin{aligned}
\text{Tax–Exempt Equiv.} &= \text{Taxable Yield}\,(1 - \text{Tax Rate}) \\
&= 10.75\% \times (1 - .28) \\
&= 10.75\% \times .72 \\
&= 7.74\%
\end{aligned}
$$

Thus, Kent would require a tax-free yield of 7.74 percent in order to have no preference between the General Motors bond and a municipal bond. In this case, the tax-free yield of 7.3 percent on the municipal bond is not sufficiently high and Kent should purchase the taxable bond.

---

taxes) are permitted as itemized deductions on the federal tax return, savings in the investor's state income tax liability from tax-free municipal bond interest will reduce deductions for state income taxes that are used to reduce federal taxes. Thus, the reduced deduction caused by paying lower state taxes will make the state income tax exemption of municipal bond interest less valuable, because the deduction is offset partially by reduced deductions in the calculation of federal taxes. When an investor uses state income taxes as an itemized deduction on the federal return, Equation 3-8 is altered slightly so that the tax equivalent yield is found as:

$$
\text{Taxable Equivalent Yield} = \frac{\text{Nontaxable Yield}}{(1 - t_f - t_s + t_f t_s)} \qquad \text{(Equation 3-10)}
$$

If the investor in the above example itemizes federal income tax deductions, the taxable equivalent yield for a tax-free municipal bond that yields 7.6 percent is

$$\frac{.076}{[1 - .31 - .06 + (.31)\,(.06)]} = \frac{.076}{(1 - .37 + .02)\quad .65} = .076$$

$$= .117, \text{ or } 11.7\%$$

Thus, the investor who itemizes deductions in computing federal income taxes loses a portion of the tax advantage of tax-free municipal interest and does not require quite as high a return on taxable securities to have no preference for either taxable or nontaxable investments. The difference in yields for an investor who itemizes deductions compared to those for an investor who does not itemize deductions for federal income tax purposes is not great, but in a world where professional portfolio managers earn their keep by improving returns by a fraction of a percent, an investor must understand how returns are affected by taxes.

The Value of the Intangible Tax Exemption

The value of exemption from a municipal bonds intangible tax depends upon the size of the tax and whether the investor utilizes intangible tax payments as an itemized deduction when computing federal income taxes. The higher the rate of the intangible tax, the more valuable is the exemption from the tax. The exemption from an intangible tax is more valuable to an investor who does not utilize the intangible tax as an itemized deduction on the federal return.

The avoidance of an intangible tax is for most investors considerably less important than the exemption from either federal or state income taxes. The burden of an intangible tax is quite small even though the tax is levied against the market value of the security as opposed to the income the security provides. Thus, avoidance of the tax is not a major consideration for most investors.

The exact calculation for determining whether it is advisable to avoid an intangible tax is somewhat more complicated than the calculations for federal and state income tax exemptions. Because of the complexity of the calculation and the smaller value of the ex-

---

Exhibit 3-14
Comparing Taxable and Nontaxable Yields
when Both Federal and State Taxes Are Considered

Beverly Howell receives a call from her broker who touts a new municipal bond issue that sells at par to provide a tax-free yield of 7.9 percent. When Beverly inquires about taxable issues, the broker replies that a taxable corporate bond of similar risk and maturity is available with a yield of 11.2 percent. Beverly is in the 31 percent federal tax bracket and resides in a state that taxes regular income at a rate of 4 percent. Because the municipal bond is issued within Beverly's state, the state will not tax her interest payments.

With Beverly's high income, she pays a significant amount of state income taxes so that she itemizes deductions on her federal tax return. She would have to pay both federal and state taxes on interest income from the corporate issue. Beverly informs the broker that she will evaluate the two bonds and call back within the hour.

To provide an equivalent after-tax return to the 7.9 percent yield offered by the municipal bond, a taxable security would have to provide the following yield:

$$\frac{\text{Tax–Free Yield}}{1 - \text{Fed Tx Rt} - \text{St Tx Rt} + (\text{Fed Tx Rt})\,(\text{St Tx Rt})}$$

$$= \frac{.079}{1 - .31 - .04 + (.31)\,(.04)}$$

$$= \frac{.079}{1 - .35 + .012} = \frac{.079}{.662} = .119 = 11.9\%$$

For Beverly, a taxable security would have to yield at least 12.3 percent to be competitive with the tax-free municipal yield of 7.9 percent. Because the taxable security offered by the broker yields only 11.2 percent, she will earn a higher after-tax return by choosing the municipal bond.

---

emption, we will forego complicating Equation 3-8 with an adjustment for the intangible tax. Roughly, an individual who purchases an asset that is exempt from an intangible tax achieves an increase in yield that is approximately equal to the rate at which the intangible tax is levied. Thus, if the intangible tax rate is one-tenth of 1 percent, the investor will need to earn an additional one-tenth of 1 percent on investments that are subject to the intangible tax. In the above example in which an investor needs a taxable return of 11.9 percent to match a nontaxable return of 7.6 percent, an intangible tax of one-tenth of 1 percent (.001 of the market value) will increase the required return on the taxable security to 12 percent.

MATURITY LENGTHS AND RATES OF RETURN

The rates of return available to municipal bond investors are very much a function of the maturity lengths of the securities. Because both maturity and return are important considerations when acquiring municipal securities, an investor should have an understanding of how the two variables are related.

Most of the time, municipal bonds with long maturities provide higher yields than municipal bonds with shorter maturities. There are a number of explanations offered for the difference in yields according to maturity. Some individuals feel that long-term securities subject investors to additional risks so that municipal bonds with longer maturities must provide higher yields to be competitive. Others who have studied the relationship between maturity length and rates of return attribute the variation in yields to differences in the demand for and supply of loanable funds. For example, if most borrowers prefer to tie down long-term funding at the same time that most lenders prefer to enter into short-term agreements, there will be a relatively large demand for long-term funds and a large supply of short-term funds. Thus, yields on long-term municipals will exceed yields on short-term municipals.

The Municipal Bond Yield Curve

The relationship between maturity and rates of return on fixed income investments is known as the *yield curve*. With yields measured on the vertical axis and maturity lengths scaled on the horizontal axis, the yield curve normally slopes upward to the right (said to be a *positively sloped* curve), because yields and maturity lengths tend to be positively related (i.e., higher yields generally prevail at longer maturity lengths). Exhibit 3-15 illustrates the yield curve that existed in early 1990 for A- rated municipal bonds.

With an upward sloping yield curve, investors are able to earn higher yields to maturity by selecting municipal bonds with longer maturities. As a rule, yields climb at a decreasing rate for maturity lengths of ten to fifteen years. After fifteen years, yields tend to flatten out so that municipal bonds with a fifteen-year maturity frequently provide about the same yield to maturity as do municipal bonds with maturities of twenty-five to thirty years.

The relationship between maturity length and yield is in constant flux. The municipal bond yield curve shifts upward or downward at the same time that the shape of the curve is changing. An upward shift indicates an increase in interest rates at all maturities. If yields on some maturities increase more than yields on other matu-

EXHIBIT 3-15
Municipal Bond Yield Curve

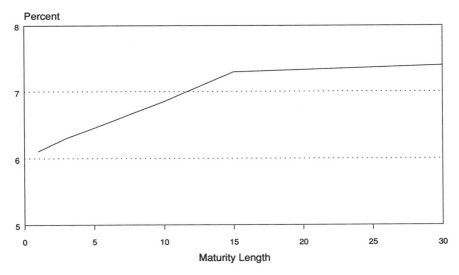

A-Rated Issues in Early 1990

rities, the shape of the yield curve is altered. A downward shift in the yield curve indicates a decrease in interest rates at all maturity levels.

Short-term interest rates tend to be much less stable than long-term interest rates so that the left side of the yield curve is subject to significantly larger fluctuations than the right side of the curve. The large fluctuations that occur in short-term interest rates are an important consideration for owners of short-term municipal bonds, because the fluctuations make it very difficult to estimate the rates at which funds can be reinvested when the bonds come due. An investor may purchase a short-term municipal bond yielding 7 percent annually over two years and discover that at reinvestment time the rate on new two-year municipals is only 5.5 percent. This risk, termed *reinvestment risk*, will be discussed at greater length in Chapter 4.

The Inverted Yield Curve

Although long-term interest rates generally exceed short-term interest rates, short-term rates occasionally rise above long-term rates to produce a yield curve that slopes downward to the right. The negative slope produces an "upside-down" curve that is frequently referred to as *inverted*. It is important to understand that an inverted yield curve is much more the exception than the rule. Because investors in municipal bonds tend to be quite sensitive to yield differences at various maturities, an inverted yield curve has a major effect on investment selections.

The most common explanation for a downward sloping yield curve is that savers and borrowers are acting on the belief that interest rates will decline. Suppliers of funds (i.e., investors) attempt to lock in existing interest rates by purchasing long-term bonds even though these bonds offer a lower yield than short-term bonds. At the same time, borrowers concentrate on short-term loans that can be refinanced when interest rates decline. Thus, during periods when interest rates are expected to decline there tends to be a large supply of long-term funds relative to short-term funds. This, in turn, puts upward pressure on short-term interest rates and downward pressure on long-term interest rates, thereby producing an inverted yield curve.

Many investors have a tendency to choose municipal securities with short maturities when short-term rates are equal to or greater than long-term rates. They make this selection based on the belief that there is no reason to assume the risks inherent in owning long-term municipal bonds when yields on short-term municipals are comparable or even higher. The problem with this reasoning is that if the expectations that brought about the inverted yield curve prove to be accurate, the choice of short-term securities may turn out to be exactly the wrong course of action.

RISKS AND RATES OF RETURN

One of the long-standing axioms of finance is that investors must accept higher levels of risk in order to earn higher rates of return. This relationship between risk and return stems from the fact that the majority of investors do not like uncertainty. As a group, investors prefer investments with known outcomes—savings accounts, Treasury bills, certificates of deposit, and high-grade municipal bonds. Because of this preference for riskless investments, investors can be induced to shift their funds away from "safe" assets toward more risky investment vehicles only when the investors are compensated with higher expected returns for doing so. Thus, investors will choose more risky municipal bonds if the increase in expected return (normally, the yield to maturity) is sufficiently above the expected return on high-grade municipals.

It is important to understand the direct relationship between risk and return, partly because an investor may be alerted to potential troubles that ordinarily would be overlooked. For example, a municipal bond that offers an unusually high yield nearly always does so for a reason; the bond may sell at a premium and be subject to being called in the near future, or the municipality may have a crumbling tax base so that future interest payments to bondholders are doubtful. Regardless of the explanation, a municipal bond with a yield to maturity that is high relative to the yields that are available on competing bonds is an indication that the market is demanding a premium and that additional investigation is warranted.

In some instances, an investor may be able to take advantage of the risk-return relationship to earn a higher rate of return. If there are risks that are deemed relatively unimportant to an individual investor, then the possibility of earning slightly higher returns for accepting these risks may be an intelligent decision. For example, municipal bonds that lack an active secondary market tend to offer higher yields to compensate for the fact that the bonds likely will be difficult to resell. An investor who purchases bonds with the intention of holding the securities until maturity may consider the lack of a secondary market relatively unimportant. Thus, the individual may pick up a fraction of a percent in yield for accepting a risk that is deemed to be of little consequence. Of course, an individual investor's circumstances may change so that what was considered unimportant at the time the municipal bond was purchased may become important at some point down the road.

Risk premiums change constantly over time. During some periods, investors are unwilling to part with their funds to purchase investments with uncertain outcomes unless they are offered a relatively large premium for assuming risk. At other times, investors are willing to purchase relatively risky bonds that offer only a slight increase in yield. The periods of relatively small risk premiums tend to be characterized by a strong economy and an optimistic mood on the part of investors. When investors are concerned about political or economic conditions, they demand greater risk premiums so that the spread in yield between ultra-safe municipal bonds and municipal bonds with a degree of risk becomes larger. All this and more will be further explained in the following chapter that is devoted exclusively to municipal bonds and risk.

Chapter
Four

THE RISKS OF OWNING
MUNICIPAL BONDS

Despite the fact that municipal bonds frequently are marketed to investors as being among the lowest risk investment alternatives, ownership of these assets can subject investors to some very important uncertainties. Even high-grade, short-term municipal bonds can produce a certain degree of risk. Understanding the risks that are inherent in owning municipal bonds is a very important component of the investment process.

Analyzing the risk of municipal bonds requires that an investor first understand the diverse variety of factors that comprise investment risk. Despite what many investors seem to believe, there is more to risk than simply the possibility that an asset may decline in market value following purchase. Assessing the riskiness of an investment must take into account the likelihood that the asset may be difficult to resell. An investor also must consider the extent to which the asset's real value may be adversely affected by inflation. And what of the differences in risk between assets that make periodic cash payments (e.g., dividend or interest payments) and assets that provide no cash payments? All of these considerations must be included in a comprehensive evaluation of an investment's riskiness.

WHAT IS RISK?

Investment risk is the uncertainty of the rate of return that will be earned during the time that a particular asset or portfolio of assets is held. The greater the uncertainty of return, the greater the riskiness of the investment position. In a few rare cases—for example, insured money market accounts, passbook savings accounts, and money market mutual funds that restrict investments to short-term U.S. government securities—the uncertainty of return is virtually nonexistent. This is also true for U.S. Treasury securities and certificates of deposit with very short maturities. However, the majority of investment alternatives—yes, even municipal bonds—can subject investors to considerable uncertainty with respect to the rate of return that will be earned.

The uncertainty of an investor's rate of return is a comprehensive concept that includes several possibilities including changes in market values, interruption of an investment's income stream, and the inability to dispose of an asset at current market value. The uncertainty of an investment's return also includes changes in an investor's purchasing power caused by unanticipated increases in the price level for goods and services. Because unexpected changes in consumer prices have the potential for devastating the real value of both the interest payments and the principal of a municipal bond portfolio, purchasing power risk will be the first cause of uncertainty addressed.

PURCHASING POWER RISK

Purchasing power risk is the uncertainty of return caused by the possibility of unexpected inflation. Inflation is a very important consideration for investors who own municipal bonds because the majority of bonds guarantee the payment of a fixed number of dollars. Even if the payments are certain to be made in full and on schedule, there is no way to determine exactly how much the payments will be worth (e.g., what the payments will buy). It is the questionable real purchasing power of the payments from municipal bonds that constitutes the purchasing power risk of owning these securities.

Nominal Versus Real Returns

Investors will sometimes forget to make an adjustment for expected changes in purchasing power when they evaluate a municipal bond's rate of return. An 8 percent coupon, $10,000 principal amount municipal bond that sells at par provides investors with an 8 percent yield regardless of whether the return is measured as the bond's current yield or yield to maturity. However, an 8 percent yield may be inadequate if an investor anticipates a 6 percent annual rate of inflation. Thus, investors always should consider potential changes in consumer prices when they evaluate the adequacy of the expected yield on a municipal bond.

The return on an investment, unadjusted for inflation, is termed the *nominal* return. The 8 percent coupon bond just discussed provides an owner with a nominal return of 8 percent. Adjusted for inflation, the rate of return is classified as the *real* return. The relationship between the real and nominal rates of return is shown as:

$$r_r = r_n - i \qquad \text{(Equation 4-1)}$$

where:

r_r =   the real rate of return
r_n =   the nominal rate of return
i =   the actual or expected rate of inflation

If municipal bonds provide a yield to maturity of 8 percent at the same time that the expected rate of inflation is 5 percent, the real rate of return is 3 percent (8 percent less 5 percent). The greater the difference between the nominal return and the rate of inflation, the greater the real rate of return from owning a municipal bond.

Although Equation 4-1 is not particularly complicated or difficult to understand, the formula conveys one of investing's most important relationships: it is not the rate of return an investor earns that is important, it is how much the rate of return exceeds the rate of inflation that determines how an investor fares. No matter what the size the investment's return is, if the nominal return does not exceed the rate of inflation, the investment is a loser because the investor will be left with less real purchasing power than before making the investment.

Exhibit 4-1
Comparing Nominal and Real Returns

Steve Parrish is a hard-working physician's assistant who has spent a career listening to doctors discuss their latest investment fiascoes. As a result of these stories, Steve has become a very conservative investor who is especially worried about inflation.

At the moment, Steve is concerned that inflation will eat away a substantial portion of the expected return from a municipal bond that is being recommended by his trusted broker, Don Simmons. Don is touting an intermediate-term municipal bond issued by Dade County, Florida, that will provide Steve with an annual after-tax return of 6.75 percent until maturity in five years. Steve is trying to figure out the real return he will earn if inflation occurs at 4.75 percent, the rate that last evening's business news reported is expected by economists.

Using Equation 4-1, Steve's real return from the municipal bond will be as follows:

$$\text{real return} = \text{nominal return} - \text{expected inflation rate}$$
$$= 6.75\% - 4.75\%$$
$$= 2\%$$

Thus, if inflation occurs as expected, Steve will slightly increase the purchasing power of his funds by buying the bonds.

Investors who earn a return of 14 percent during a period when the annual rate of inflation is 12 percent are worse off than investors who earn a return of 6 percent during a period when inflation is 2 percent. This is a difficult concept for many investors to swallow, especially when interest rates have declined from unusually high levels.

Purchasing Power Risk and Municipal Bond Investments

Because investors must be concerned about real returns and borrowers about the real cost of borrowing, the pricing and the resulting yields for municipal bonds incorporates some consensus expectation for inflation. As long as inflation occurs at the expected rate, both borrowers and investors earn the real returns that they anticipated when the bonds and the monies change hands. It is when the rate of inflation turns out to be different than the level anticipated that investors and borrowers either unexpectedly benefit or are injured.

If the rate of inflation turns out to be lower than expected, then the real cost of money is greater than anticipated by borrowers and investors. Municipal bond investors win in such an environment because the real rate of return (the nominal rate adjusted for the rate of inflation) is higher than expected and the purchasing power of both the interest payments, and the principal repayment is greater than had been anticipated at the time the bonds were purchased. Conversely, if inflation turns out to be greater than expected, the borrower and not the investor (actually, the lender) benefits. In this instance, the municipalities' real cost of borrowing and the investors' real rate of return are lower than had been anticipated.

Investors who own municipal bonds are at substantial risk from potential changes in purchasing power because the payments made to bondholders are fixed in amount. No matter how much consumer prices rise over the period of time that a municipal bond is held, the owner of the bond receives the same amount of money every six months. As inflation persists year after year, succeeding payments have less and less purchasing power.

A certain amount, or perhaps all of the depreciation in purchasing power, has been anticipated by both the investor and borrower at the time the bonds changed hands. The anticipated change in purchasing power was included in the original yield on the bond. It is when purchasing power declines at a greater-than-expected rate that the real return is less than had been anticipated when the security was purchased.

Suppose an investor who purchases an 8 percent coupon municipal bond anticipates 5 percent inflation but discovers within a year after the date of purchase that inflation has crept upward until consumer prices are increasing at an annual rate of 10 percent. In this example, the fixed interest payments and eventual principal

---

Exhibit 4-2
Winners and Losers from Unexpected Inflation

If inflation is less than expected

The municipal bond owner benefits because the real return is greater than anticipated at the time the bond was purchased.

The municipal borrower is hurt because the real cost of funds is greater than expected when the money was borrowed.

If inflation is greater than expected

The municipal bond owner is hurt because the real return is less than anticipated at the time the bond was purchased.

The municipal borrower benefits because the real cost of funds is less than anticipated when the money was borrowed.

---

repayment depreciate in value far more rapidly than the investor anticipated. The depreciation in purchasing power occurs so rapidly, in fact, that interest payments are not enough to make up for the rate at which consumer prices are rising. With inflation at a rate that is higher than the nominal return on the bond, the investor will actually lose purchasing power during each period that the bond is owned.

Exhibit 4-3 illustrates the deteriorating purchasing power of the payments received on a $5,000 principal amount 8 percent coupon bond over a life of twenty years at different levels of inflation. The sum of the bottom of each column indicates the total purchasing power from all the payments, adjusted for inflation, that will accrue to the owner of the bond. Only when the rate of inflation is less than the yield on the bond (in this case, 8 percent annually), will the purchasing power of the payments exceed the purchasing power that was foregone when the bond was acquired.

For example, if annual inflation is 4 percent, the owner of the bond will receive payments with a total purchasing power of $7,717.20 over the entire twenty years that the bond is held. When the yield on the bond is exactly the same as the rate of inflation, the aggregate purchasing power of all the interest payments plus the principal will equal exactly the purchasing power that was given up by the buyer when the bond was purchased. A municipal bond with a yield to maturity that matches the rate of inflation permits an investor to retain, but not to increase, the purchasing power of the money that is invested.

Certain types of assets tend to provide investors with a hedge against purchasing power risk. For example, some companies are able to increase earnings during periods of rising consumer prices, and they pass along a portion of the earnings increases in the form of higher dividends for common stockholders. Likewise, investors in real assets such as real estate and precious metals are likely to benefit from unexpectedly high inflation that will result in an increase in the market values of these assets by more than the rate of inflation.

Unfortunately, long-term, fixed-income investments, of which municipal bonds are an example, do not normally provide investors with increasing payouts or increasing market values to offset the ravages of unexpected inflation. Large increases in consumer prices over an extended period of time will devastate the real value of a fixed payment or a series of fixed payments.

There is another important inflation-related consideration for municipal bondholders. Because both borrowers and investors judge the adequacy of a bond's yield partly on the basis of expected inflation, changes in inflationary expectations will impact upon the market value of a municipal bond. In other words, not only does inflation eat away at the real value of the payments received by the owner of a municipal bond, but increases in inflationary expectations will result in even greater losses because of higher nominal interest rates and lower bond prices. The importance of market rates of interest to the value of all fixed income securities introduces a second major risk to the owners of municipal bonds—the risk of interest rate changes.

INTEREST RATE RISK

There is an inverse relationship between interest rates and municipal bond prices. Rising interest rates force the market values of

Exhibit 4-3
Purchasing Power of
a Municipal Bond's Interest and Principal
at Various Inflation Rates
(8 percent coupon, $5,000 principal, 20-year maturity)

Year of	Rate of Inflation			
Payment	0%	4%	8%	12%
1	$ 400.00	$ 384.80	$ 370.40	$ 357.20
2	$ 400.00	370.00	342.80	318.80
3	$ 400.00	355.60	317.80	284.80
4	$ 400.00	342.00	294.00	254.40
5	$ 400.00	328.80	272.40	226.80
6	$ 400.00	316.00	252.00	202.80
7	$ 400.00	304.00	233.20	180.80
8	$ 400.00	292.40	216.00	161.60
9	$ 400.00	281.20	200.00	144.40
10	$ 400.00	270.40	185.20	128.80
11	$ 400.00	260.00	171.60	114.80
12	$ 400.00	250.00	158.80	102.80
13	$ 400.00	240.00	147.20	91.60
14	$ 400.00	230.80	136.00	82.00
15	$ 400.00	222.00	126.00	73.20
16	$ 400.00	213.60	116.80	65.20
17	$ 400.00	205.20	108.00	58.40
18	$ 400.00	197.60	100.00	52.00
19	$ 400.00	190.00	92.80	46.40
20[1]	$ 5,400.00	2,644.80	1,161.00	561.60
Total	$13,000.00	$7,717.20	$5,001.80[2]	$3,508.40

[1]Year 20 values include both the final interest payment and the $5,000 return of principal.

[2]This total is overstated by $1.80 because of rounding.

outstanding bonds downward, and falling interest rates push municipal bond prices upward. The greater the change in interest rates, the greater the change in bond prices—although bonds with different maturities and different coupons are affected to different degrees.

The cause of the inverse relationship between market rates of interest and the market prices of outstanding municipal bonds is relatively easy to understand. An investor will be unwilling to pay face value for a municipal bond that has an 8 percent coupon if municipal bonds of similar maturity and risk are being offered in the primary market with yields of 10 percent. Municipal bonds with 8 percent coupons are able to compete in a market environment with 10 percent coupon bonds only if the 8 percent bonds sell at prices that offer potential buyers a competitive yield. Thus, if market rates of interest rise, outstanding municipal bonds must decline in price in order to provide investors with a yield that is competitive with new bonds. The more that new bonds yield (e.g., the more that market rates of interest rise), the more that existing bonds must decline in price to provide the return that investors demand.

Interest rate risk for investors who own municipal bonds stems from the possibility that interest rates will increase following the date that a bond is purchased, thereby reducing the security's market value. Even an investor planning to hold a bond until maturity suffers from rising interest rates. Although only paper losses will result if the security is not sold, the investor will continue to earn a return that is less than the return that could be earned on alternative securities. The greater a municipal bond's price change for a given change in interest rates, the greater the interest rate risk from owning the bond.

Interest rate risk for investors owning municipal bonds is a function of both the bond's maturity length and coupon size. In general, the shorter the maturity and the larger the coupon, the lower the interest rate risk of owning a particular bond. Conversely, the longer the maturity of a bond and the lower its coupon size, the greater the change in the bond's market value for a given change in interest rates and the greater the risk of owning the bond.

The Importance of Maturity Length

The maturity length of a municipal bond is a major factor in determining the extent to which the bond's market value is influenced by changes in market rates of interest. Short-term bonds—debt securities with maturities of up to two or three years—are affected little by changes in market rates of interest. At the same time, the market values of municipal bonds with maturities of twenty years and over are strongly affected by changes in market rates of interest. Thus, the interest rate risk of a municipal bond is directly related to the maturity length of the bond.

The maturity of a municipal bond indicates the length of time before the bond's principal will be repaid and funds equal to the face value of the bond can be reinvested by the investor. The longer the time until the principal is repaid, the greater the cumulative losses to a bond's owner during a period when higher interest rates are available on alternate investments. A municipal bond with a long maturity extracts a large penalty from its owner in an environment of rising interest rates.

Suppose two $1,000 par, 8 percent coupon bonds, one with a twenty-year maturity and the other with a five-year maturity, are trading in a market with a flat yield curve (yields at all maturity lengths are the same) that is at a level of 10 percent. Both bonds will sell for less than their $1,000 face value because the coupons on the bonds are lower than the market rate of interest. However, the longer maturity length of the twenty-year bond will cause that bond to sell at a price of only $4,150 compared to the five-year bond which will sell in the secondary market at a price of $4,625. The reason for the price difference between the two bonds is that the principal on the short-term bond will be returned a full fifteen years before the principal on the long-term bond will be repaid. Thus, funds invested in the five-year bond will be available for reinvestment at the higher interest rate much sooner than funds that are invested in the twenty-year bond.

On the positive side, in a market environment of declining interest rates, bonds with long maturities increase more in market value than do bonds with short maturities. An investor expecting lower interest rates may want to purchase a municipal bond with a long maturity in order to pin down the current high rate. If the forecast

---

Exhibit 4-4
Maturity Length and Price Changes

Two years ago, Yankton, South Dakota, sold an issue of tax-exempt bonds that included only two maturities: five years and twenty-five years after the date of issue. The five-year bonds carried a 6 percent coupon, and the twenty-five-year bonds had an 8 percent coupon. Bonds of both maturities were sold at par in units of $5,000. Following the date of issue, market rates of interest began to rise until, after two years, rates were a full percentage point above the rates that existed when Yankton's bonds were issued.

In the new interest-rate environment, the bonds will have the following market value (using Equation 3-2 from Chapter 2):

Short-term bond (Three years remaining until maturity and selling in the secondary market to yield 7 percent)

$$\text{Price} = \frac{\$300}{(1.07)^1} + \frac{\$300}{(1.07)^2} + \frac{\$300}{(1.07)^3} + \frac{\$5,000}{(1.07)^3}$$

$$= \$787.20 + \$4,080.00 = \$4,867.20$$

Long-term bond (Twenty-three years remaining until maturity and selling in the secondary market to yield 9 percent)

$$\text{Price} = \frac{\$400}{(1.09)^1} + \frac{\$400}{(1.09)^2} + \cdots + \frac{\$400}{(1.9)^{23}} + \frac{\$5,000}{(1.09)^{23}}$$

$$= \$3,832.09 + \$690.00 = \$4,522.08$$

Thus, the long-term bonds will decline substantially more in market value than will the short-term bonds.

---

for lower interest rates proves to be accurate, the bondholder will continue to earn the higher interest rate on the principal amount of the bond. Because the bond will pay such a large amount of annual interest for many years in the future, there will be a greater increase in the market price for the long-term bond than for a bond with a short maturity.

Exhibit 4-5 illustrates the prices at which 8 percent coupon municipal bonds with various maturities will sell when the market rate of interest is 6 percent, 8 percent, and 10 percent, respectively. The curve that slopes upward to the right indicates the market values for 8 percent coupon bonds of various maturities when the market of interest is 6 percent. Because the coupon on the bonds is greater than the market rate of interest, the bonds will sell at a premium with the size of the premiums increasing at longer maturities.

The curve that slopes downward to the right indicates the market values for 8 percent coupon bonds of various maturities when the market rate of interest is 10 percent. With a market rate of interest that is greater than the coupon on the bonds, the market values of the bonds must be less than their face value. Again, the size of the discount depends upon the maturity length of each bond; the longer the maturity, the greater the discount.

The third curve, actually a horizontal line at the center of Exhibit 4-5, indicates the price at which 8 percent coupon bonds with differing maturities will sell in a market that demands an 8 percent return. The horizontal line illustrates that the bonds must sell at par.

The Importance of Coupon Size

Interest rate risk is inversely related to the size of a municipal bond's coupon. Thus, the market values of municipal bonds with relatively high coupons are less affected by market interest rate movements than the market values of municipal bonds with relatively low coupon rates. The inverse relationship between coupon size and interest rate risk is caused by the fact that the bonds with high coupons accelerate the investor's cash flow with relatively large interest payments that are available for reinvestment at the current market rate of interest.

The sooner funds are received and can be reinvested, the less interest rate changes affect the market value of an asset. Essentially, the explanation for the importance of a bond's coupon size is identical to the explanation outlining the importance of maturity length—

Exhibit 4-5
Maturity Length and Interest Rate Risk

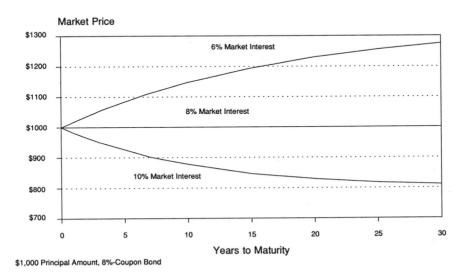

$1,000 Principal Amount, 8%-Coupon Bond

faster and bigger cash flows dampen the swings in an asset's market value caused by interest rate changes.

Suppose two municipal bonds with identical maturities and similar risk are trading in a market that demands a yield of 10 percent for fixed income securities with similar investment characteristics. One bond was issued by the state of Nevada with an 8 percent coupon while the second bond was issued by the city of Minneapolis with a 14 percent coupon. Both securities now trade in the secondary market.

The Nevada bond with a coupon rate that is lower than the market rate of interest must sell at a discount to face value while the Minneapolis bond with a coupon higher than the market rate will sell at a premium to its face value. The size of both the discount and the premium will depend upon the size and date of the principal repayments. Assuming that each bond has a ten-year maturity and a $5,000 principal and that neither security may be called by the issuer prior to maturity, the Nevada bond should trade at a price of approximately $4,388 while the 14 percent Minneapolis bond should sell for about $6,231.50.

It is relatively easy to recognize that the higher coupon Minneapolis bond returns a greater proportion of cash in the form of interest payments and that these cash payments begin flowing almost immediately following the date of purchase. The owner of the Minneapolis bond will be able to reinvest relatively large amounts of cash at whatever the going rate of interest happens to be only a short time after the bond is acquired.

On the other hand, the 8 percent coupon Nevada bond makes relatively skimpy periodic interest payments ($400 annually versus $700 annually for the Minneapolis bond) so that the return of principal comprises a comparatively larger portion of the bond's market value and a larger amount of its aggregate cash payouts. For example, the present value of the Nevada bond's principal (the $5,000 principal discounted at 10 percent for ten years) is 44 percent of the bond's current market value of $4,388, while the Minneapolis bond's principal is only 31 percent of that bond's market value of $6,231.50. Because the Nevada bond requires owners to wait ten years before the large single principal payment can be reinvested, the market price of the bond is strongly affected by changes in interest rates that occur following the date of purchase.

Exhibit 4-6 illustrates the relationship between market value and the market rate of interest for each of the two bonds just discussed. The 14 percent coupon Minneapolis bond will always sell at a price higher than the 8 percent coupon Nevada bond, and the Minneapolis bond can be expected to have larger absolute price movements for a given change in the market rate of interest. However, the lower-coupon Nevada bond produces *proportionately* greater price movements so that investors will find themselves subject to greater gains and losses from interest rate movements for an equal dollar investment than investors in the Minneapolis bond. The greater relative price movements, in turn, result in a greater uncertainty regarding the rate of return, thus, subjecting the investor to greater interest rate risk.

The above example noted that with a 10 percent market rate of interest the 14 percent Minneapolis bond should sell for $6,231.50,

Exhibit 4-6
Coupon Size and Interest Rate

Market Price

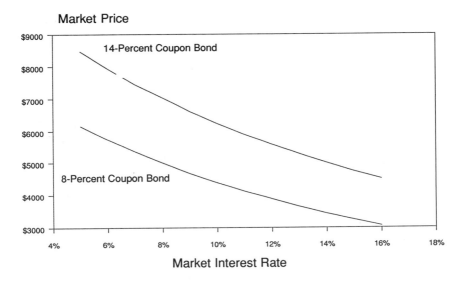

Market Interest Rate

and the 8 percent coupon Nevada bond should sell for $4,388. At these prices, each bond provides investors with a 10 percent yield. Now suppose the economic environment changes, and the market rate of interest increases to 14 percent (assume the same ten-year maturity). Because the Minneapolis bond's coupon rate is now equal to the market rate of interest, this bond should decline in price until it sells for its face value of $5,000. The increase in interest will cause the 8 percent coupon Nevada bond to decrease to a price of $3,436.40. In percentage terms, the higher coupon Minneapolis bond decreases in price by 19.8 percent ($1,231.50/$6,231.50) while the lower-coupon Nevada bond falls in price by 21.7 percent ($951.60/$4,388). The larger percentage decline for the lower coupon bond illustrates that the low-coupon bond will subject investors to greater interest rate risk.

Exhibit 4-7
The Importance of a Municipal Bond's Coupon Size

Dot Young, a wealthy entrepreneur, has been a steady buyer of municipal bonds over the past decade. One day Dot's friendly broker, Phil Smith, telephones to tell her about two municipal bonds that are available in the secondary market. Both bonds trade in $5,000 denominations and are priced to provide a yield to maturity of 7 percent. In addition, both bonds have ten-year maturities. One bond has a 12 percent coupon and sells for $6,654.40. The second bond has a 7 percent coupon and sells at par. Dot thinks there is a chance that interest rates will rise to 8 percent within a year, and she wishes to determine which bond would provide the greatest protection from the expected increase in interest rates.

	12% Coupon	7% Coupon
Price in 7% Market	$6,754.40	$5,000.00
Price in 8% Market	6,248.20	4,686.45
Loss in Market Value	506.20	323.55
Interest Received	600.00	350.00
Profit (Interest − Loss)	93.80	26.45
Rate of Return (Profit/Beginning Price)	1.4 %	0.5 %

Thus, the 12 percent coupon bond will provide Dot with a higher rate of return.

REINVESTMENT RISK

Reinvestment risk refers to the uncertainty of return that is caused by an unknown rate at which cash flows can be reinvested. The greater the uncertainty as to the return that will be earned from reinvesting a municipal bond's cash flows (e.g., payments of inter-est and principal), the greater the reinvestment risk from holding a particular bond.

In reality, higher market rates of interest benefit bondholders who have cash flows available to reinvest because higher interest rates increase the investor's rate of return. The reinvestment risk to an investor who purchases a municipal bond is that interest pay-ments and/or the principal repayment will have to be reinvested at a reduced rate of return because of a decline in the market rate of interest following the bond's purchase.

Earlier chapters discussed the call feature contained in the bor-rowing agreements of many municipal bond issues. A call feature can add to an investor's reinvestment risk, because it may make it more difficult for an investor to determine the length of the interest stream due to uncertainty as to when the principal will be repaid by the borrower. Thus, the municipal bondholder is uncertain as to when reinvestment will be required as well as to the rate that will be earned on reinvested funds.

Not all municipal bonds with call features produce additional risks for investors. A call price for a bond selling in the secondary market at a large premium to both its principal and its call price is likely to establish the bond's life. Thus, there is no doubt that the bond will be called. For bonds with a low coupon that sell at a large discount from face value, the existence of a call feature is unimport-ant because the bonds almost certainly will not be called. In each instance, the call feature causes no additional uncertainty for the investor so that the feature does not produce additional risk.

Callable bonds that sell reasonably close to their par values and call prices may well be called prior to their scheduled maturities. If this is the case, the call feature causes a major uncertainty because the lives of the bonds depend upon future movements in the mar-ket rate of interest, something that is extremely difficult—some say impossible—to forecast accurately. Unless an investor is able to project the level of future interest rates accurately, the lives of many callable bonds are unknown, and the investor's future earnings stream is uncertain.

The Importance of Reinvestment Risk

The significance of reinvestment risk depends upon the use a particular investor intends to make of the cash flows that are received. For example, investors who plan to utilize all of a bond's cash payments for acquiring goods and services will be unconcerned about the rate at which flows can be reinvested because there will be no reinvestment.

When an investor plans to utilize interest payments for consumption but intends to reinvest the principal at maturity in order to produce a continuing flow of income, reinvestment risk is applicable only to the bond's principal repayment. On the other hand, an investor who purchases a municipal bond with the intention of reinvesting all cash flows—both interest and principal—will be subjected to uncertain returns on a long stream of cash payments.

A retiree who subsists on an income that is drawn primarily from investments should be particularly concerned about reinvestment risk. Suppose, for example, that an individual has accumulated $200,000 and that the funds currently are invested in 8 percent coupon municipal bonds with an average maturity of three years. The annual income of $16,000 ($200,000 x .08) may prove adequate at the time the securities are purchased, but what will happen if, at the time the bonds mature in three years, the market rate of interest has declined to 6 percent? The reduced annual income of $12,000 from the reinvested principal may be insufficient to provide anything other than subsistence living.

Now consider the importance of the reinvestment rate to someone who is reinvesting all cash flows in order to accumulate a sum of money for some specific purpose—an early retirement or the purchase of an exotic sports car. Because both interest and principal are being rolled over continually into new income-producing investments, the reinvestment rate becomes crucial in determining whether the goal will be achieved. Over a long period of time, a reduction in the reinvestment rate will result in a significantly smaller accumulation of funds with a reduced likelihood that the goal will be attained.

Exhibit 4-8 illustrates the importance of the reinvestment rate to someone who plans to reinvest all interest payments. The example assumes that interest payments from a $5,000 principal 10 percent

Exhibit 4-8
Importance of the Reinvestment Rate

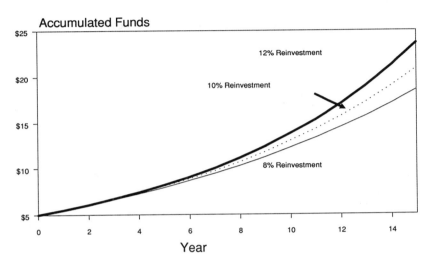

10%-Coupon, $5,000 Principal Bond

coupon bond are reinvested at an annual rate of either 8 percent, 10 percent, or 12 percent over the bond's fifteen-year maturity. The principal and the accumulation of both the bond's interest payments and the earnings from reinvested interest (e.g., interest earned from reinvested interest) at each of the three reinvestment rates are represented by the three curves displayed in the exhibit. The illustration shows that after fifteen years of reinvesting interest, an 8 percent reinvestment rate will result in the accumulation of $18,576 compared to accumulations of $20,886 and $23,640 at reinvestment rates of 10 percent and 12 percent, respectively.

Reducing Reinvestment Risk

Municipal bonds with characteristics that minimize an investor's exposure to interest rate risk—high coupons and either short maturities or the likelihood of early calls—are the same securities that maximize an investor's exposure to reinvestment risk. A municipal bond that produces a rapid series of sizable cash flows, either through large interest payments or a quick principal repayment, is subject to relatively small price movements from changes in market interest rates at the same time that the bond presents its owner with a reinvestment problem.

Reinvestment risk is reduced most easily by selecting municipal bonds with long maturities and no call features. And because low-coupon bonds produce less interest income that must be reinvested, they create less uncertainty. For example, a 5 percent coupon bond issued ten years ago with an original maturity of thirty years (twenty years currently remaining until maturity) subjects an investor to significantly less reinvestment risk than does a 9 percent coupon bond with a maturity of ten years. Although municipal bonds with coupons that are below the market interest rate will sell at a discount from face value, the yield to maturity on the bonds should be competitive with the yield that is provided by higher-coupon bonds that are part of new issues.

FINANCIAL RISK

Financial risk for the owner of a municipal bond is the uncertainty of return caused by the possibility that the bond's guarantor (generally the issuer, although the payments on some issues also are guaranteed by insurance companies or banks) may be unable to meet the financial commitment relative to the bond. The commitment, of course, is to make the interest payments and principal repayments that the issuer has guaranteed to the bondholders.

The Importance of Financial Risk

If investors consider only a single type of risk when they contemplate the acquisition of an investment asset, this risk is likely to be of the financial variety. Individuals often view risk as the possibility that their income will be slashed and/or their principal will be lost. These possible outcomes, in fact, are what financial risk is all about.

Consider the difference between owning the municipal bonds of a public hospital and municipal bonds issued by the state of Virginia. Most hospitals are caught between escalating expenses and restrictions on reimbursements from insurance companies and the federal government. Combined with a decrease in occupancy rates, the resulting squeeze on operating margins has transformed hospitals into financially risky enterprises. At the other end of the spectrum, even though states have been pinched by rapidly rising expenses—including higher health costs for their employees and the poor—and by the need to repair and expand their capital infrastructures, these government entities have available to them the great revenue enhancer, taxation. When states run into a financial squeeze the customary response is to raise taxes, a solution that hospitals are unable to duplicate.

The wide gap between the financial stability of most public hospitals and that of state governments produces an equally large difference in the degree of financial risk faced by investors who become the creditors of these institutions. In the comparison noted above, bonds issued by the state of Virginia subject investors to significantly less financial risk than do the bonds issued by nearly any public hospital in the country. The payments to holders of the Virginia bonds are more likely to be paid in full and on time.

While some types of risk may be of little consequence to particular investors (for example, reinvestment risk to an investor who plans to spend both interest and principal payments), financial risk is a concern for virtually every investor. Investors who acquire assets in order to generate current income, to produce capital appreciation, to meet long-term goals, or to achieve short-term goals are concerned about the possibility that interest payments will be interrupted or principal will remain unpaid.

Coping with Financial Risk

Most investors are unable to judge accurately the financial risk that results from owning a particular municipal bond. The ability to obtain and evaluate the necessary data simply is beyond the available time and training and beyond the intellectual capabilities of the vast majority of investors. An alternative to making a personal judgment about financial risk is to rely upon an independent authority that undertakes the analysis and makes available the results to investors.

Independent rating companies routinely evaluate and grade municipal bonds. Moody's Investor Service and Standard and Poor's Corporation, the two largest bond rating agencies, are in the business of providing an analysis of the financial risks that accompany particular issues of municipal bonds and other fixed income investments. Although prospective issuers are required to pay the agencies a fee to obtain a rating for their bonds—a practice that some observers feel constitutes a possible conflict of interest—history indicates that the ratings have proven to be of substantial benefit to investors who are involved in the municipal bond market.

The risk rating categories of bonds vary somewhat among the rating firms, but the top three or four categories generally are reserved for bonds that qualify as high quality, or *investment grade.* An investment grade rating indicates that the issuer's or guarantor's ability to service the debt is strong. Of course, the spectrum of investment grade is fairly wide, so that some bonds qualifying as investment grade are of such high quality that they are considered similar to U.S. Government obligations while other investment-grade municipal bonds that are in a lower rung of the investment grade category are judged to be less secure with respect to interest and principal payments.

Gradings supplied by the independent rating agencies are good indicators to utilize when judging the financial risk involved in a particular municipal bond. As a rule, investors should limit their selections to bonds graded A or higher, and they should shy away from bonds that are not rated at all. Absence of rating does not necessarily indicate that a bond subjects an investor to substantial financial risk, but ignoring the possible danger involved in acquiring a bond with no rating is simply not worth the risk.

The financial risk of a particular municipal bond can change subsequent to the date that a bond is acquired. Perhaps the best example of this change is the rapid decline in the financial status of states and many municipalities in the southwestern United States following the plunge in oil prices in the 1980s. The decreased demand for petroleum resulted in an increase in the financial risk for investors holding municipal bonds from many of the issuers in this region of the country. Reduced ratings by Moody's and Standard and Poor's for existing bonds as well as for new bonds were common during this period of regional economic decline. A detailed breakdown of the municipal bond ratings that are supplied by Moody's and Standard and Poor's is in Appendix C.

LIQUIDITY RISK

Liquidity risk refers to a municipal bondholder's uncertain return due to the possibility that the bond will be difficult to turn into cash prior to maturity. A bond's lack of liquidity generally is caused by a dearth of trading in the secondary market. The lack of trading means that there are few bids from dealers or other investors so that a broker has to solicit a buyer for the bonds. The bottom line is that a bondholder may have to accept a reduced price (compared to the price at which the bond should trade under normal circumstances) should it become necessary to sell the bond prior to the scheduled maturity.

Liquidity risk generally is less of a concern for investors who hold financial assets than it is for individuals who own tangible assets such as real estate, stamps, coins, and antiques. Most financial assets are homogeneous in that one asset can be substituted easily for another asset with identical characteristics. Thus, 100 shares of General Motors common stock is identical to any other 100 of shares of General Motors common stock. Tens of thousands of GM shares trade daily and each of these shares is identical in detail and value to every other share of General Motors common stock. The huge number of identical units of most financial assets facilitates the trading of these assets in the secondary market.

Because there are many thousands of different municipal bond issues, and because these issues are frequently issued in comparatively small dollar amounts, there is a relatively inactive secondary market for many municipal issues. Reduced liquidity in municipal bonds also is caused by the fact that many investors purchase these securities in the primary market with the intention of holding them until maturity. Thus, a significant portion of many municipal bond issues never trades in the secondary market. The remaining portion of most municipal issues is not traded with any regularity.

The bottom line is that an investor assembling a portfolio of individual municipal issues may have to absorb a discount if it becomes necessary to sell some or all of the securities prior to their scheduled maturities. This doesn't mean that investors should avoid the purchase of individual issues of municipal bonds. It does mean that investors must consider the likelihood that bonds may have to be liquidated prior to maturity. If the likelihood of an early sale is great, the investor may be better served by selecting bonds with short maturities (an action that is likely to result in the selection of bonds with lower yields to maturity) or by substituting tax-free mutual funds or investment trusts for a portfolio of individual bond issues (a topic discussed in Chapter 6).

A SUMMARY OF RISK AND MUNICIPAL BOND OWNERSHIP

Even though municipal bonds generally are merchandised as investments with virtually no risks, this chapter has indicated that there are several potential hazards that should concern investors interested in acquiring these securities. The importance of the risks varies significantly depending on the investment characteristics of a particular municipal bond (e.g., maturity length, call feature, coupon rate, issuer, and so forth) and the goals and characteristics of the investor.

Risks associated with municipal bond ownership range from loss of purchasing power to the inability to sell a bond without accepting a large price discount. Realizing that owning any municipal bond subjects an investor to some degree of risk, an individual must determine which risks are most relevant to his or her individual circumstances. In certain instances, one or more individual risks may be relatively unimportant for a particular investor. At the same time, one of the other risks may be a very important consideration.

Investors should understand that the risk of individual investments cannot be measured in isolation. Rather, the risk of an asset is important to the extent to which it affects the riskiness of an investor's overall portfolio. Investors must view a municipal bond in terms of how it affects the overall investment position.

In portfolios that are heavily weighted with municipal issues, investors can reduce most risks by including bonds with a wide variety of maturities and issuers. Selecting bonds with a variety of maturities provides a certain degree of protection from both reinvestment risk and interest-rate risk. Diversifying among different issuers helps reduce business and financial risks—uncertainties that tend to be unique to specific issuers.

Chapter
Five

BUILDING A MUNICIPAL BOND PORTFOLIO

An investor discussing municipal bond investments generally is referring to the purchase or ownership of individual municipal bond issues. That is, the investor recently may have purchased $10,000 in principal amount of general obligation bonds issued by Andersonville, Indiana. The bonds pay semi-annual interest and specify a maturity date on which the $10,000 principal will be returned.

Purchasing individual bond issues is not the only way—and, indeed, not necessarily the best way—for every investor to participate in the municipal bond market. Chapter 6 will discuss the advantages and disadvantages of indirectly acquiring municipal bonds through the purchase of mutual fund shares and trust units, two widely popular investment vehicles that offer tax-exempt income. Both alternatives to direct bond purchases offer some very real advantages for many of the investors who seek tax-exempt income.

Still, accumulating a portfolio of tax-exempt municipal bonds has its good points, not the least of which is the confidence of an investor who knows that some big cities and states owe her money. Maybe movie star Kim Basinger can purchase the small Georgia town of Braselton, but the municipal bond investor can brag that the city of Atlanta owes her some big money, and on a long-term basis.

ADVANTAGES OF INVESTING IN
INDIVIDUAL ISSUES OF MUNICIPAL BONDS

Ownership of individual municipal bonds provides more concrete benefits than the satisfaction an investor feels every six months upon receiving a check drawn on the account of New York City or Seattle. Perhaps the most important benefit from acquiring individual issues of municipal bonds is that an investor earns a higher rate of return than from bonds acquired indirectly through shares of a mutual fund or a unit trust.

Another advantage to acquiring tax-exempt income through the purchase of individual municipal bond issues is an investor can assemble a portfolio of bonds that provides desired cash flows. Purchasing individual bonds permits an individual to choose securities with maturities and interest payment dates that are tailored to personal needs.

Also, acquiring individual issues of municipal bonds permits an investor to put together a portfolio of bonds that provides the best fit from the standpoint of risk. There are disadvantages to acquiring individual issues of municipal bonds, of course, but the negatives will be saved for the following section. Now is the time for a discussion of the positive points of individual bond selection.

Individual Bonds Can Provide a Higher Rate of Return

It is difficult to get someone to do something for nothing, especially in the financial world where participants earning six- and seven-figure annual incomes speak in terms of profit margins, return on capital, and the bottom line. Any time an investor is offered something for nothing, it is time for the investor to turn and run.

Both investment companies and trust sponsors put together and manage (trusts are generally unmanaged) municipal bond portfolios in order to earn a profit for themselves. The profit motive doesn't mean that these firms don't serve the public good, of course, for mutual funds and unit trusts provide investors with valuable alternatives to purchasing bonds directly. However, there is no getting around the fact that the sponsors of both investment companies and municipal bond trusts provide this service for a fee, and that the fee is paid by those who take advantage of the service.

Mutual fund managers charge shareholders an annual fee to cover the costs of operating the fund. In addition, many funds have sales charges that involve fees either at the time shares are purchased or at the time shares are redeemed. Annual management fees frequently amount to between 0.5 percent and 0.75 percent of a fund's assets. Sales fees, if they exist, are on top of management fees and are sometimes partially hidden in the form of annual 12b-1 charges. Fees charged by mutual funds and unit trusts are discussed in more detail in Chapter 6. Fees charged by investment companies result in a direct reduction in the yield the investor could have earned by purchasing bonds directly.

Building an individualized portfolio of municipal bonds permits an investor to avoid the management and sales fees of mutual funds and the selling charges established by the sponsors of municipal bond trusts. Depending upon the size of a mutual fund's annual management fee and whether the fund also levies a sales or liquidation fee, the reduction in yield can amount to 1 percent or more annually when an investor buys through a trust or investment company. Considering that municipal bonds provided annual tax-exempt yields of from 7 to 8 percent during the early 1990s, the loss of a full percentage point in annual return is a considerable sacrifice on the part of the investor. The sacrifice may be worth it, of course, but the loss of yield from paying professionals to assemble and manage a municipal bond portfolio can take a substantial bite out of the returns earned by an investor.

It is not only the freedom from sales and management fees that permits an investor in individual municipal bond issues to earn higher returns. Individual investors may occasionally stumble onto bonds that most institutional investors ordinarily would avoid. For example, a bond issue may not have been rated by a rating agency simply because the issue was relatively small in amount, and the issuer decided not to incur the expense of obtaining a rating. Because unrated bonds often are spurned by institutional investors, it is likely that an individual investor who selectively adds these bonds to a portfolio can obtain a higher yield without accepting a great deal of additional risk.

Likewise, investors can sometimes find municipal bonds trading in the secondary market that are less desirable because of the small size of the offering. For example, a bond dealer may offer a small bond position ($5,000 to $15,000 principal amount) at a slightly higher yield than larger positions simply to clear the bonds from the firm's inventory. The high yield (low price) offered to a buyer doesn't mean that the dealer is doing the investor a favor because the dealer likely has purchased this same issue at a discounted price. An institution would not wish to become involved in the issue because of the small amount of funds involved. Many individual investors also shun small positions in individual issues simply because they would have to acquire a very large number of individual bond issues if their portfolios are of a substantial size.

One other potential yield advantage of individual municipal bond issues stems from an investor's ability to concentrate on the bonds that provide the greatest tax advantage. For example, an investor who resides in a state that taxes interest from out-of-state municipal bonds can build a portfolio of in-state bonds that provides interest income free of both federal and state taxation. Single-state funds and trusts are available for investors who reside in states with large populations and high tax rates; however, the number of these funds is limited and acquisition of the funds is likely to entail higher fees. For investors residing in states with moderate taxes and small populations, there generally are no specialized funds available.

Likewise, an investor who is not concerned about the alternative minimum tax can accumulate a diversified portfolio of municipal bonds that are subject to this tax. Because municipal bonds subject to the alternative minimum tax (AMT) generally offer relatively high yields, AMT bonds are preferred by many investors who have few tax preference items and therefore do not pay the tax.

An Individualized Portfolio Can Provide a More Desirable Cash Flow Stream

One of the significant advantages to building a portfolio of individual municipal bond issues is that an investor can select bonds that provide the most suitable cash flows for a particular investor's needs. That is, an investor can acquire the bonds that have the "right" coupons and maturities.

Suppose, for example, that an investor decides to sock away funds for a child's college education. Assuming that college funds will not be required for ten years, the investor may wish to select municipal bonds with ten-year maturities, or, better yet, four issues of bonds that mature in four consecutive years beginning in ten years (with the wishful thinking that the child will not be become a "long-term" student). It could well be that this investor would be best served by acquiring zero-coupon municipal bonds so that there will be no concern about reinvesting semi-annual interest payments.

Likewise, a couple saving for retirement in twenty years can concentrate on acquiring bonds with coupons and maturities that are best suited for that goal. The couple may wish to put together a portfolio of individual municipal bonds that mature over a period of years so that both interest and principal can be used for living expenses. Both the years until retirement and the couple's life expectancies at the time of retirement will play major roles in the pattern of cash flows that is desired.

At the opposite extreme, suppose an individual is approaching retirement and that a sufficient amount of retirement income (employer pension, social security, rental income, etc.) will be available to push the individual into a high tax bracket. In this case, the individual may wish to acquire municipal bonds that provide the highest possible current income subject to limitations on risk. To maximize current income, the investor should consider high-coupon municipal bonds that sell at premiums to par. Premium bonds may be best suited for this individual even though the bonds are likely to be called prior to maturity and will produce a capital loss. The call dates and respective yields to call become crucial factors in determining if individual bond issues are desirable investments.

Acquiring tax-exempt income through the purchase of mutual funds or unit trusts does not provide an investor with the same ability to nail down cash flows as does the acquisition of individual bond issues. In the case of trusts, an investor has great difficulty in estimating when bonds will be called and, thus, when principal may be returned. In the case of mutual funds, there are no scheduled dates when principal will be returned. Rather, proceeds from redeemed bonds are reinvested in new securities. Although shares can be sold back to the fund, there is no way to determine in advance the price that will be received, because the value of a fund's shares will depend on the market rate of interest at the time the shares are sold.

Individual Bond Issues Can Produce a Portfolio with Superior Risk Characteristics

An investor who seeks tax-exempt income through purchase of individual issues of municipal bonds is able to select bonds that best fit the investor's particular risk profile. Thus, an individual can select a bond that offers the most desirable maturity, call feature, rating, and issuer. For example, an investor can select municipal bonds that geographically diversify a portfolio or that stagger the maturities of portfolio's securities.

An investor who has no immediate need for periodic interest payments and who is concerned that interest payments will have to be reinvested at unpredictable interest rates may wish to assemble a portfolio of zero-coupon bonds. Because zero-coupon bonds make no interest payments, there is no interest that needs to be reinvested.

An investor may wish to assemble a portfolio of bonds that *ladders* maturities. That is, each bond added to the portfolio has a maturity that is different from the maturities of the bonds already owned. A portfolio containing bonds that mature over a range of years moderates the investor's exposure to interest rate risk (the risk of changing bond values caused by shifts in interest rates) at the same time that bonds with longer maturities moderate the investor's exposure to reinvestment risk. Depending upon whether an individual investor views interest rate risk or reinvestment risk as more important, additions to a portfolio can stress bonds with either short-term or long-term maturities.

DISADVANTAGES OF INVESTING IN INDIVIDUAL ISSUES OF MUNICIPAL BONDS

Ready-made portfolios of tax-exempt bonds exist for a reason. The popularity of mutual funds and unit trusts that specialize in providing investors with tax-exempt income indicates that many investors prefer this route to investing in individual issues of municipal bonds. Part of the reason that funds and trusts are popular is that brokers frequently sell these investments harder. The commission structure and reduced investment requirement on the part of investors make funds and trusts a better product than individual bonds issues for brokers to promote. At the same time, there are some very good reasons that honest brokers will steer customers away from individual issues of municipal bonds.

Buying Individual Issues Requires Substantial Capital

Because municipal bonds trade in denominations of $5,000, an investor must accumulate at least $5,000 to purchase a single bond. (It is possible to invest less if a bond is purchased in the secondary market at a discount.) This fairly substantial investment contrasts with trusts that generally trade in $1,000 units and mutual funds that are sold in even smaller amounts. Of course, for individuals with substantial funds to invest, minimum investments of $5,000 create no difficulty. Many wealthier investors purchase municipal bonds in minimum lots of $25,000 and more.

With incremental investments of $5,000 per municipal bond, many investors must accumulate funds over time in order to raise sufficient capital to purchase even a single bond. This means that unless the investor is willing to accept the relatively low returns that are provided by tax-exempt money market funds, he or she will have to forgo tax-exempt income while accumulating sufficient funds for investment in a municipal bond. Such a process is certainly less convenient than socking away money in a tax-exempt mutual fund on a regular basis.

Adequate Diversification May Be Difficult to Achieve

Experts suggest that individual investors need to own at least seven to nine municipal bond issues in order to have a portfolio that is adequately diversified. Thus, an investor will require a portfolio amounting to at least $40,000 to $50,000 to achieve proper diversification. Many investors can only accumulate this amount of money over a lengthy period. The long period of time that many investors require to put together a diversified portfolio means that these same investors are subjecting themselves to substantial risk until their task is complete. For example, an investor who is able to put aside only $5,000 annually and who decides to use the funds to purchase individual municipal bonds will be exposed to substantial amounts of risk for seven to eight years until a diversified portfolio of bonds can be assembled.

Even a portfolio with a sufficient number of bonds may exhibit inadequate diversification. For example, an investor may concentrate on municipal bonds from a limited geographic region or bonds whose timely payments of interest and principal are dependent on the economic health of a limited number of businesses. Individual investors frequently acquire bonds without taking time to consider how a new acquisition fits into the existing portfolio. The investor's broker spots some bonds in the secondary market or receives a bulletin on a new municipal issue the firm will be underwriting. Knowing the kind of bonds the investor tends to buy, the broker calls and makes a pitch for the bonds. If the investor is only an occasional buyer, the broker probably hasn't spent much time evaluating what bonds would provide the best fit with the client's account. Rather, the broker has considered what bonds the investor is most likely to find acceptable.

Without adequate portfolio diversification, one or two unfavorable events that occur simultaneously can produce disastrous investment results. Adequate diversification depends upon more than simply owning a prescribed number of bond issues.

Individual Bonds May Be Difficult to Sell Prior to Maturity

An investor who attempts to sell a $5,000 municipal bond for the first time is likely to be in for an unpleasant surprise. The surprise isn't that there will be no market—there is always a buyer at the right price. The problem is that the right price may be substantially lower than the investor expects and, indeed, lower than seems fair given market rates of interest at the time of the sale.

Municipal bonds tend to trade in principal amounts of at least $35,000 so that a bond position amounting to less than $25,000 may have to be liquidated at a discount from the price than a larger lot would bring. Thus, an investor who diversifies a municipal bond portfolio by accumulating $5,000 principal amounts of a number of bond issues ends up with a portfolio that lacks liquidity.

Of course, if an investor is fairly certain that all of the bonds in a portfolio will be held until maturity, the lack of liquidity is less important. In fact, an individual who cares little about the portfolio's liquidity may be able to take advantage of being a small investor by obtaining favorable prices on small lots of municipal bonds in the secondary market that other investors or dealers are having difficulty selling.

Because the municipal bond market is so fragmented it is difficult for an individual investor to add to a particular bond position with more bonds of the same issue. Thus, an individual who purchased $5,000 principal amount of an 8 percent coupon California Housing Authority issue of 1982 maturing in 2012 will have great difficulty locating identical additional bonds. Because it is generally very difficult to locate bonds in the secondary market that are identical to bonds that are already owned, it is virtually impossible for an investor to turn an odd lot into a round lot. A more likely scenario is that an investor wishing to turn an odd lot into a round lot will have to sell an odd lot and acquire a round lot of bonds with similar maturity, coupon, and risk characteristics.

Maintaining a Large Portfolio Can Be a Chore

It may seem that no sane person would complain about keeping track of his or her investments, especially when the investments are relatively uncomplicated assets like municipal bonds. Periodically checking on semi-annual interest payments and maturity dates would seem to be a trifling task for someone who is earning tax-exempt income.

Still, over a period of years an individual investor can accumulate a significant number of different municipal bond issues so that record-keeping starts to become a drudgery. Not only must the investor make certain that interest payments are received on time, but maturity dates and call dates must be monitored, and interest and principal will have to be reinvested. This task can be especially grinding if there is only a nominal amount of principal for each of the bonds held in the portfolio. An individual purchasing one or two $5,000 bonds each year will accumulate up to twenty different issues over the course of a decade.

Record-keeping is more burdensome if the investor has taken delivery of the bonds. The investor will have to deposit interest checks and withdraw bond certificates from the lockbox each time a bond matures or is called. As the certificate and the resulting payment on the bond are in transit, some interest might be lost.

Keeping bonds in street name can reduce an investor's record-keeping, because the brokerage firm will record interest payments and take care of bond redemptions. Depending upon the firm that is utilized, cash payments from interest and redemptions may be swept automatically into a money market account so that interest is earned until the funds are reinvested. Even in this case there may be some delay, however, as some firms sweep cash into money market accounts weekly rather than daily. Exhibit 5-1 summarizes some of the advantages for investors of allowing brokerage firms to keep custody of their municipal bonds.

When an investor utilizes several brokerage firms for municipal bond purchases, keeping bonds in street name can become somewhat cumbersome and, perhaps, expensive. Assuming that bonds will be left at the firms where they are purchased, an investor will end up with several accounts, each with a portfolio that appears to have little direction because it is only part of the whole picture. Each of these accounts must be monitored by the investor. While maintaining three or four accounts may be an improvement over tracking ten to fifteen individual bond issues, multiple accounts can nonetheless prove to be bothersome.

Multiple brokerage accounts also can result in additional costs to the investor. An increasing number of brokerage firms have begun levying annual charges against "inactive accounts" that range from $50 to $100. Having multiple accounts increases the likelihood that an investor will be hit with one or more fees during the year.

An Individual May Overpay for Bonds

Professional investors and bond traders get a feel for the market so that they have a fairly accurate estimate of the price at which a

---

Exhibit 5-1
Advantages of Keeping Municipal Bonds in Street Name

- Brokerage firm keeps track of early redemptions from calls and regular redemptions at maturity.
- The investor can sell securities more easily because no delivery is required.
- Brokerage firm collects interest payments. Many firms automatically sweep these payments into a money market fund.
- Bonds are available as collateral for loans, often at rates that are significantly below the rates charged on credit card balances.
- Monthly statements show portfolio holdings, bond values, and receipt of interest payments.
- Brokerage firm carries insurance against theft or loss of certificate (but not declines in market value). Insurance coverage varies with firm.

---

particular bond should trade at a given point in time. Because of the huge number of municipal bond issues that trade in the secondary market, even professionals may have to perform some background work in order to get a firm grip on the fundamentals of a particular bond issue, but the experience of being involved in the market on a full-time basis brings a familiarity that makes getting a "fair deal" likely.

Compared to professional investors, individual investors who only occasionally enter the municipal bond market tend to be much more at the mercy of the people with whom they are doing business. Because there tends to be very little mercy in this line of work, it is not unusual for an individual to pay several points more than the price that an institution might pay. Overpaying several points for bonds means that an individual investor may lose most of the savings that result from not having to pay management and distribution fees to an investment company or the sponsor of a unit trust.

Part of the problem that the individual investor encounters stems from the fact that dealers and brokers deal in bonds on a net basis. That is, a customer is told the yield and price but not the dealer's markup or the broker's commission. All of the markups and commissions are built into the quoted price and, essentially, hidden from view. Thus, the individual investor has no idea of the size of the spread between the bid and ask on a particular bond.

Most individual investors have a minimal amount of current information concerning the municipal bond market and what offerings are available. As a result, the individual bond buyer often has minimal knowledge with which to determine if the price being quoted on a particular municipal bond is "fair." Closely related to the lack of knowledge concerning the overall municipal bond market is the fact that, at the time the purchase is being contemplated, the investor is likely to be doing business with a single firm so that only the bonds that particular firm has in inventory are being considered. It would not be unusual for another broker-dealer to be offering bonds with virtually identical characteristics at a slightly different price at the same time.

CONSIDERATIONS IN PURCHASING MUNICIPAL BONDS

Although different investors have disparate goals that call for varying investment strategies, there are some general guidelines concerning municipal bond investments that are applicable to the majority of individual situations. Individuals sometimes operate under exceptional circumstances, of course. Still, most investors can enter the municipal bond market armed with some basic guidelines.

Purchase Municipal Bonds in the Primary Market

To avoid the possibility of being overcharged for municipal bonds in the secondary market, an investor can purchase bonds that are offered as part of new issues. Purchasing bonds in the primary market allows the individual to avoid paying unknown dealer markups at the same time that it provides some assurance that the yield the investor is receiving is pretty much the yield the market is demanding at the time of the transaction.

It is less likely that an investor will be overcharged when purchasing new issues of municipal bonds because all buyers, big and small, pay the same price for the bonds. Thus, an investor who purchases $10,000 principal amount of a new issue will pay the same price and receive the same yield as another investor who purchases $100,000 principal amount of the same issue.

Another advantage with respect to the yields offered on new issues is that issuers and investment bankers often will offer yields that are slightly above yields available on bonds in the secondary market in order to ensure that the bonds will receive an enthusiastic reception from investors.

At the same time that all the players are paying the same price for bonds, the issuer is picking up the tab for selling expenses and dealer markups. Sales fees are part of the costs incurred by borrowers bringing new issues to market, so that investors who purchase securities in the primary market avoid the commissions and markups of transactions in the secondary market. Saving one or two points ($10 to $20 per $1,000 principal amount) on several municipal bond purchases annually can result in substantial savings over the years.

Although purchasing municipal bonds at either a discount or a premium to par can each produce certain advantages (i.e., a discount bond is less likely to be called prior to maturity), there is something appealing about purchasing bonds at face value. If an investor desires to acquire bonds at par, then the primary market offers a preferred avenue to building a portfolio because most municipal bonds are brought to market at par. Acquiring a bond at face value makes it easy to calculate yield (the yield to maturity is equal to the coupon rate), simplifies keeping track of either realized or paper gains and losses, and makes it less likely that an investor will be surprised by an unexpected call by the issuer.

When acquiring municipal bonds in the primary market, the buyer probably will be able to obtain a copy of the official statement that describes the issue. Once bonds have been brought to market and begin trading in the secondary market, official statements are difficult to find. Investors are still able to obtain information on call dates, yield to call, rating, and several other pertinent items concerning the bond, but they won't have access to all of an issue's details.

Seek Out a Broker Who Knows Municipal Bonds

Brokers can generate more commissions by devoting their time to customers who trade stocks or become involved in futures and options. Equities and options frequently are bought to be sold while municipal bonds often are purchased by investors who plan to hold the securities until maturity. Not only is there minimal turnover in many municipal bond portfolios, the broker doesn't even earn commissions when bonds in the portfolio mature (although a commission will result if the funds received at redemption are reinvested). Because of the reduced financial incentives, many brokers tend to spend their time researching and selling common stocks and options and become involved in the municipal bond market only when specifically requested to do so by a customer.

Brokers now are required to have at least some knowledge of so many new and complicated investment products that they simply do not have enough hours in the day to perform all of the necessary tasks. Some of these uncompleted tasks might include keeping on top of the new issues market in municipals, regularly surveying the firm's municipal inventory, or learning about the small differences in details relating to municipal bond issues that can give the investor a slight edge in a very competitive market.

Brokers who execute only occasional customer trades in municipal bonds tend not to be on top of the municipal bond market. An investor with a broker who is not on top of the market might receive insufficient information and incorrect advice, both of which can be very dangerous to most individual investors.

Investors must make certain that the firms represented by brokers devote substantial resources to the municipal bond business. Having an account with a firm that underwrites new issues and that maintains a substantial inventory of secondary bonds gives an investor more options with respect to bond selection. It is also more likely that a firm that devotes resources to municipal bonds will have brokers who are knowledgeable about tax-exempt securities.

Purchase Municipal Bonds Under the Assumption That the Bonds Will Be Held to Maturity

It is generally a good policy to purchase a municipal bond with the intention that the bond will be held until maturity. That is, it is best to select maturities on the basis of when funds are likely to be needed rather than on the basis of interest rate differences between maturities. Purchasing long-term municipal bonds in order to gain twenty-five to fifty extra basis points (one-quarter to one-half of 1 percent) in yield when the invested funds are likely to be required many years prior to maturity is asking for trouble.

Trying to earn an extra quarter or half of a percent annually when a bond might have to be liquidated at a substantial loss is foolish greed. The danger of having to liquidate a bond at a loss is especially great for individuals who purchase small lots that may be difficult to dispose in the secondary market.

Even when an investor expects interest rates to decline, acquiring a bond with a maturity that is substantially longer than the expected holding period for the bond is generally a mistake. It would be nice to think that individual investors are clever enough to forecast interest rates accurately so as to take advantage of interest rate changes and earn profits from changing security values in addition to tax-exempt interest payments. Unfortunately, history suggests that accurately forecasting interest rates is a task even beyond the abilities of most professionals.

Stick with High-Grade Municipal Bonds

Individual investors generally make a mistake when they reach for extra yield on bonds that incur additional risk. Groping for higher yields is most likely to occur during a period of declining interest rates when investors have become accustomed to interest rates that are no longer available for bonds with the same degree of riskiness. In an attempt to maintain the higher yields, investors sometimes are tempted to acquire bonds that exhibit a degree of risk that formerly they would not have found acceptable.

Most individuals are unable to monitor the day-to-day health of an issuer so that a marginal credit can hit a tailspin before many bondholders are aware of the change. A high-grade municipal bond downgraded by one of the rating agencies is not as potentially disastrous as a municipal bond downgraded from a rating that is already considered marginal. Individuals should stick with high-grade securities: municipal bonds having a minimum rating of A and, preferably, bonds rated AA or AAA.

Many individual municipal bond issues improve in quality even though the ratings remain unchanged. However, individual investors seldom have either the time or the expertise to ferret out bonds that have too low a rating and, thus, may be underpriced in the secondary market. Thus, for the purposes of most investors, a rating by one of the rating agencies is an adequate measure of a bond's credit risk.

Investigate the Municipal Yield Curve When Selecting a Bond to Purchase

Chapter 3 discussed the concept of the yield curve—the relationship at a point in time between yield and maturity length. The yield curve for municipal bonds (indeed, for all bonds) generally slopes upward to the right; bonds with longer maturities provide investors with higher yields. Only occasionally does the yield curve become flat or slope downward to the right.

Even though the yield curve normally slopes upward to the right, the slope of the curve is not constant. The slope is generally steepest for short-term and intermediate-term securities. At maturities of twelve to fifteen years, the curve often begins to flatten so that bonds with twenty-five-year maturities yield only slightly more than bonds with fifteen-year maturities. This is only a generality, however, and the point in the curve where the slope becomes less steep (sometimes called the *kink*) is constantly shifting. In fact, as Exhibit 5-2 illustrates, the yield curve is likely to have multiple kinks at one time. Also, the kink can be at a different point in the municipal bond market than in the market for corporate bonds or for government bonds.

If an investor who is in the market to purchase a municipal bond is undecided about what maturity to select, a bond with a maturity length that is at or close to the point of the kink in the yield curve provides what is likely to be the best available yield-maturity combination at that particular time. An investor who is not sure at what maturity length yields begin increasing at a reduced rate should feel free to ask a broker who can quickly determine the point of the kink by scanning the scale of a new bond issue.

The yield curve certainly is not an investor's only consideration in selecting municipal bonds. For example, the next section discusses the importance of putting together a portfolio of bonds with maturities that are spread over a wide range of years. Still, an investor always should consider the shape of the yield curve when purchasing a bond.

Consider a Bond Issue's Call Feature

Individual investors frequently fail to investigate the call feature of a bond issue. This omission is less likely for bonds that sell at a premium in the secondary market because premium bonds are frequently quoted on a yield-to-call basis. Also, an investor with any experience in the bond market is virtually certain to ask for information on the call date and call price when a bond is selling at a premium. It doesn't take investors very long to learn the importance of a call feature on a premium bond.

However, when bonds are purchased at a discount in the secondary market or purchased at par as part of a new-issue, investors frequently fail to investigate call features. In some instances a broker will call an investor's attention to a discount bond in the secondary market without first investigating the bond's call feature. And because the bond is selling at a discount, an investor is more likely to forget that a call feature still can be very important, especially if the bond is selling only slightly below par.

Call features for bonds that sell in the primary market often are overlooked because of the call protection that most newly issued municipal bonds offer to buyers. However, the protection from a call on even newly issued municipal bonds generally is limited so that any major decline in interest rates will cause the investor to reinvest funds at a reduced yield in as short a period as five years. For individuals who invest in housing bonds, there may be virtu-

---

Exhibit 5-2
Interest Rate Scale on a Municipal Bond Issue

In August 1986, the Hospital Authority of Gwinnett County, Georgia, issued slightly over $46 million principal amount of tax-exempt refunding revenue anticipation certificates. The issue included $14 million principal amount of serial certificates and $32 million of term certificates. Yields and maturities for the serial portion of the issue were distributed as follows:

Maturity	Yield	Maturity	Yield	Maturity	Yield
1987	4.75%	1992	6.20%	1997	6.80%
1988	5.25	1993	6.40	1998	6.90
1989	5.50	1994	6.50	1999	7.00
1990	5.75	1995	6.60	2000	7.10
1991	6.00	1996	6.70		

There are actually three kinks in the yield curve for the Gwinnett issue: at maturities of 1988, 1991, and 1993. The kinks result from a .50 percent increment in annual yields between maturities in 1987 and 1988, .25 percent increments from 1988 to 1991, .20 percent increments from 1991 to 1993, and .10 percent increments from 1993 until the last serial bond in 2000.

An investor who "buys the kink" would purchase bonds maturing in 1988, 1991, or 1993 because of the decline in yield increments that follow each of these maturities. Beyond each of these maturities the additional reward is reduced when an investor accepts a longer maturity.

---

ally no protection from a call, and the bonds may be called within a year or two after the issue date.

CONSIDERATIONS IN BUILDING
A MUNICIPAL BOND PORTFOLIO

Investors should follow some common-sense guidelines when purchasing individual bonds. Useful guidelines will result in the acquisition of tax-exempt securities that best meet an individual investor's financial goals. Individuals also should consider certain policies when putting together a portfolio of municipal bonds. To a large extent, the guidelines that apply to a portfolio are merely an extension of the rules that apply to the selection of individual securities. Still, investors should carefully consider some of the guidelines applicable to municipal bond portfolios.

A Portfolio Must Consider an Investor's Goals and Assets

Just as an investor should consider the municipal bonds that are already owned when evaluating the acquisition of a new bond, the investor must consider other asset holdings when putting together a municipal bond portfolio. For example, few investors should devote their entire investment portfolio to municipal bonds. Granted, the safety record and tax exemptions make municipal bonds very appealing. However, concentrating too heavily on municipal bonds has some serious drawbacks.

One of the major disadvantages of concentrating too heavily on fixed income securities of all kinds stems from the possibility that unexpected inflation will eat away at the real value of interest and principal until little real purchasing power remains. It is often difficult to imagine an environment of rapid inflation after experiencing several years of relatively stable prices, but economic trends are subject to sudden, and unexpected changes and stability can turn quickly into chaos.

Ladder Maturities

Changing interest rates create two avenues for municipal bondholder losses; rising interest rates cause declining market values for bonds that are already owned, and falling interest rates cause investors to earn reduced returns on reinvested interest payments and bond redemptions. Thus, the investor stands to lose regardless of which direction interest rates move. An optimist might look at interest rate movements from the opposite side—rising interest rates allow an investor to earn increased returns from reinvested funds while falling interest rates result in capital gains from in-

creased bond values. Because most individual investors who purchase municipal bonds do so for the safety, stable income, and tax
benefits, the importance of potential losses from interest rate
changes probably outweighs the importance of potential gains from
these same changes.

Exotic securities and sophisticated methods are available to
hedge against losses from fluctuating interest rates. For the majority
of individual investors who are building municipal bond portfolios,
however, the simplest and best hedge is to acquire a number of
bond issues that cover a wide range of maturities. Thus, one year an
investor might purchase $10,000 principal amount of Atlanta Gas
Light bonds maturing in 2006 and the next year purchase $10,000
principal amount of Louisiana Fuel Tax Revenue Bonds maturing
in 2007. Purchasing bonds that mature consecutively is termed
laddering.

An investor does not have to acquire bonds with maturities that
are only a single year removed from bonds that he or she already
owns, of course. The investor should consider the yields available at
different maturities (i.e., the shape of the yield curve). During the
early stages of portfolio-building, this presents no problem because
so few maturities will have been filled. However, at some point the
investor should be willing to sacrifice some yield in order to balance the maturities of bonds that will be held in the portfolio.

Beware of Relying Too Heavily on Insured Bonds or Bonds with Letters of Credit

Chapter 2 discussed the growing importance of letters of credit
(LOC) and insurance guarantees as credit enhancements on new
issues of municipal bonds. The bottom line for municipal borrowers
is that the expense of obtaining an insurance guarantee or an LOC
is more than offset by the savings in interest costs derived from the
credit enhancement.

Although an added credit is to the bondholder's advantage, an
AAA rating secured as a result of credit enhancement is not necessarily the same as an AAA rating obtained solely on the basis of the
issuer's creditworthiness. The difference in risk between the two
categories of municipal bonds is evidenced by the gap in yields—

bonds rated AAA without credit enhancements tend to carry lower yields than bonds rated AAA because of insurance or letters of credit.

The issue of financial safety is most worrisome in light of the potential consequences of a period of severe economic distress—an event that may be unlikely, but that is certainly not out of the realm of possibility. Private guarantees (as opposed to government guarantees) from financial institutions generally function as intended as long as losses remain random and relatively isolated. A flawed state or local project that provides collateral for a revenue bond and an occasional school district that finds itself unable to meet its financial obligations are events for which letters of credit and insurance company guarantees are adequate protection. However, there is a limit to the losses than can be sustained by a financial institution. The catastrophic losses and subsequent collapse of hundreds of savings and loans—institutions that were once considered among the country's strongest—prove that financial institutions cannot withstand all adversities.

The point of this section is not to scare readers into believing that an economic catastrophe is in the works or that insured municipals should be avoided. Rather, investors should consider diversification of a municipal portfolio to include different credit enhancements as well as different issuers. A limited amount of insured bonds in a portfolio is fine, but building an entire portfolio on the faith of several banks or insurance concerns may well turn out to be a mistake. If an investor is a conservative soul for whom a top credit rating is a primary concern, a portion of the investor's portfolio should include bonds that earned an AAA rating on the strength of the issuer's credits. In the event of a catastrophe, the taxing power of a state is likely to prove more secure than the promise of a bank that may well have become overextended in granting letters of credit.

Don't Diversify to the Extreme

While investors in municipal bonds initially have difficulty achieving diversification, over time a portfolio of bonds may actually become over-diversified. That is, a portfolio may become loaded down with so many different bond issues that the investor has difficulty keeping up with interest payments, maturities, call dates, and market values of all the securities.

After a point, adding more bond issues does little to improve diversification. Once a portfolio's holdings exceed a dozen or so issues, there is little added incentive to diversify more. This assumes, of course, that bonds within the portfolio are themselves diversified. Piling one bond issue of the Santa Fe School Authority on top of an earlier issue from the same credit is not diversification.

One obvious method for reducing the number of issues in a portfolio is to invest a greater amount of funds in each bond issue. Rather than purchasing $5,000 or $10,000 principal amount of bonds, an investor can delay purchases until $20,000 or, preferably, $25,000 can be invested. This strategy will require longer periods between investments and result in fewer issues in a portfolio.

Another tactic for maintaining a reasonable number of municipal bond issues is to add funds to the principal that is reinvested when bonds in a portfolio mature. That is, when a $5,000 principal amount municipal bond matures or is called, an investor can add $5,000 or $10,000 in extra funds and purchase a greater principal amount of replacement bonds. Over time, the investor will increase the dollar size of the portfolio without increasing the number of bond issues contained in the portfolio. If ten or so different bond issues have been acquired so that maturities occur in consecutive years, the process of upgrading the size of the portfolio without a corresponding increase in the number of issues will be relatively easy to accomplish.

Chapter
Six

TAX-EXEMPT MUTUAL FUNDS AND UNIT TRUSTS

There are several alternatives for persons who wish to acquire shelter. Individuals can purchase detached single-family homes, one-story or multi-story condominiums, or units in cooperative apartments, or they can become full-time motor home vagabonds and tour the United States in a home on wheels. Each of these choices offers a type of shelter with its own particular advantages and disadvantages that range from low cost and minimum maintenance to potentially bothersome noise. Just as there are several methods available for acquiring shelter, there is more than one method available for investors to invest in municipal bonds.

THE DISADVANTAGES OF PURCHASING INDIVIDUAL BONDS

The previous chapter discussed the considerations for an individual investor contemplating the construction of a municipal bond portfolio. There are a number of prerequisites to pursuing a successful strategy for accumulating individual issues of municipal bonds—a brokerage firm with the resources to support the investor's needs (e.g., research, underwriting new issues, etc.) and a broker who is sufficiently knowledgeable about municipal bonds to provide use-

ful advice are minimum requirements. Although each of these requirements already has been discussed in some detail, it is still
useful to briefly recall some of the problems involved in putting
together a portfolio of municipal bonds.

The Problem of Diversification

One of the significant disadvantages for most individual investors
who wish to invest in tax-exempt municipal bonds is the formida-
ble amount of funds required to construct a properly diversified
portfolio. Nearly all municipal bonds are issued and trade in $5,000
denominations (as opposed to corporate bonds that trade in $1,000
principal amounts) and multiples thereof. Thus, even a single purchase requires an outlay of $5,000, a substantial sum of money for
many investors.

Most professional investment advisors recommend at least seven
to nine different bond issues for adequate diversification. The im-
plication for the individual investor is that it will take a minimum
of $40,000 to $50,000 to have an adequately diversified portfolio of
municipal bonds. Because many individuals find it possible to accumulate this amount of funds only over a lengthy period of time,
they expose themselves to substantial risks until adequate diversification is achieved. Alternatively, these investors must delay their
purchases of municipal bonds until sufficient funds have been accumulated so that a diversified portfolio can be attained with $50,000
or purchased at one time.

The Problem of Liquidity

Acquiring minimum amounts of individual bonds presents no
liquidity problems if an investor is relatively certain that the securities will be held until maturity. However, if there is some likelihood
that bonds may need to be liquidated prior to maturity, the investor
may have to take a substantial discount when bonds are sold. The
reason is that while municipal bonds are denominated in $5,000
amounts, the normal unit of trading for these bonds is $25,000. A
trade involving municipal bonds with a face amount under $25,000
is likely to require that the seller accept a price that is less than the

market price that would be received for a round lot trade in the same security.

A related problem for individuals who acquire municipal bonds in relatively small amounts is that a portfolio may eventually include so many different issues that the investor finds it difficult to keep track of what is owned and what the portfolio is doing. For example, an individual who acquires a single $5,000 bond every six months will end up with twenty bonds in a period of ten years. At some point an investor will own so many different issues that keeping track of interest payments, maturity dates, call features, and bond values will become a burden.

Let it never be said that the investment community is short on ideas. Where there are funds to invest, there is an investment product to vacuum up the monies. For investors with modest sums of money to invest and a desire for tax-exempt income, there is a way to acquire a diversified portfolio of municipal bonds at the same time that adequate liquidity is maintained. In fact, there are two major investment vehicles that can be utilized to accomplish these feats. Although many investors seem to believe that both vehicles are essentially identical, each alternative has its own advantages and disadvantages. Different investors who have different investment patterns and different investment needs will attribute differing degrees of importance to the advantages and disadvantages of each investment vehicle.

TAX-EXEMPT MUTUAL FUNDS

A popular method for acquiring an instantly diversified portfolio of securities is to invest in the shares of a mutual fund. Mutual funds have been developed to appeal to virtually every investment taste, no matter how offbeat and bizarre. Funds sold to the public include those with portfolios that are limited to common stocks, portfolios that are limited to bonds, and portfolios that include both stocks and bonds (called *balanced funds*). If that isn't good enough, there are mutual funds that specialize in growth stocks, mutual funds that specialize in the stocks of energy companies, and mutual funds that invest only in the stocks of corporations in specific countries. And, of course, there are mutual funds that specialize in tax-exempt municipal bonds.

How Mutual Funds Are Structured

Mutual funds sell shares of stock in order to raise capital for investment in other securities. The particular kinds of securities that a fund purchases will fall within limits specified by the fund's objectives. Thus, rather than investing stockholders' money in buildings, real estate, or machinery, mutual funds invest in stocks and bonds. Likewise, while many companies make money for their stockholders by doing things such as generating and selling electricity, manufacturing tires, or operating television stations, a mutual fund attempts to make a profit for its shareholders by investing in securities that appreciate in value (sometimes) and/or that shower the fund with dividend or interest payments.

Mutual funds that provide investors with above-average returns (compared to the overall stock market or to other mutual funds) tend to attract new investors in addition to generating additional investments from existing shareholders. The resulting influx of new monies will cause the mutual funds to grow and the fund managers' income to rise. Thus, most fund managers are constantly attempting to earn returns that exceed the returns investors could earn by owning shares in competing funds or by investing in individual securities.

For mutual funds that specialize in common stocks, the competition to produce higher returns frequently results in active buying and selling of stocks in an attempt to produce capital gains. For the managers of municipal bond mutual funds, the competition results in an attempt to produce higher tax-exempt yields that are earned from interest payments on the bonds held by the funds.

Special laws exempt the income mutual funds receive from dividends, interest, and realized gains on securities from taxation as long as the funds pass through a minimum portion (for practical purposes, virtually all) of these income items to their own shareholders. The shareholders of the mutual funds then are required to report this income on their own tax returns. Thus, a mutual fund serves as a conduit that passes earnings through to its own investors who must declare the payments as income (if the income received by the fund is not tax-exempt). The justification for the lack of taxation on income earned by the mutual fund is that this income is taxed to the shareholders, and it is unjust to tax the same income twice.

For mutual funds that hold only tax-exempt municipal bonds, the interest income passed through to the fund's shareholders remains free of federal taxation. Essentially, the tax status of these payments made to the shareholders is identical to the status of the interest payments received by the fund. State taxation of payments received from a municipal bond fund depends upon the laws of the state where a fund owner resides. Owners of municipal bond mutual funds who reside in states that tax the interest from municipal bonds issued outside the state will be required to report payments from mutual funds as taxable income for state purposes.

Mutual funds not only differ from ordinary corporations in terms of taxation. Funds also are organized so that investors are continually able to purchase either new shares or cash in existing shares. Because new shares are always available from the fund which also stands ready to redeem the shares of any stockholder who wishes to sell, there is no secondary market in the shares of mutual funds. That is, there is no market in which shareholders of a mutual fund can sell their shares to other investors. With a central organization (e.g., the fund) that continually buys and sells shares, there is no need for a secondary market in which buyers and sellers would be required to pay a broker to locate one another.

The Value of Mutual Fund Shares

The total market value of all the securities that a mutual fund owns divided by the total fund shares that are in investors' hands is the fund's *net asset value (NAV)*.

If the overall market value of the shares owned by a mutual fund increases, with no accompanying increase in the number of outstanding shares, there will be an increase in the net asset value of the fund's own shares. Thus, if the shares of the six companies owned by the fund in Exhibit 6-1 double in market value to a total of $388,000, the mutual fund's NAV also will double to

---

Exhibit 6-1
Calculation of Mutual Fund's Net Asset Value

Stock	Shares Owned by Fund	Current Price	Value
Parrish Air Modeling	1,000	$45.00	$ 45,000
Howell's Car Care	800	25.00	20,000
Moore Music & Dance	5,000	10.00	50,000
Young's Realty	2,000	15.00	30,000
Krebs' Transit Co.	1,200	20.00	24,000
Stanley Saxophones	2,500	10.00	25,000
Total fund assets			$194,000

If the mutual fund has 10,000 of its own shares outstanding, the net asset value per share is calculated as follows:

$$NAV = \frac{\text{Market Value of the Fund's Assets}}{\text{Shares of the Fund Outstanding}}$$

$$= \frac{\$194,000}{10,000 \text{ shares}} = \$19.40$$

$388,000/10,000 shares, or $38.80 per share. It is this new net asset value that is applicable to owners of the fund who wish to liquidate their shares and to investors who desire to purchase shares in the fund.

Mutual funds that limit their holdings to tax-exempt municipal bonds differ from stock funds only in the type of assets they own. Rather than investing in common stocks or a combination of common stocks and bonds, tax-exempt municipal bond funds invest only in municipal bonds. Because municipal bonds tend to have more stable market values (fluctuate less in price) than common stocks, the net asset values of municipal bond funds do not fluctuate nearly as much as do the net asset values of most stock funds. This doesn't mean that municipal bond funds do not fluctuate in value, however, because they do fluctuate, and an investor who

Exhibit 6-2
Calculation of a Municipal Bond Fund's Net Asset Value

Bond	Principal Amount	Current Price *	Value
Valdosta, GA 9s00	$250,000	95	$ 237,500
State of Nevada 8s98	300,000	90	270,000
Vandewalker, TX 10s05	200,000	103	206,000
Rushville, IN 8s05	400,000	88	352,000
Yankton, SD 12s98	200,000	110	220,000
Beuther, MI 7s08	250,000	80	200,000
Wilkinson, NJ 10s07	300,000	104	312,000
Total fund assets			$2,863,000

If the municipal bond fund has 100,000 shares outstanding, the fund's net asset value per share is calculated as follows:

$$\text{NAV} = \frac{\text{Market Value of the Fund's Bonds}}{\text{Shares of Fund Oustanding}}$$

$$= \frac{\$2,863,000}{100,000 \text{ shares}}$$

$$= \$28.63 \text{ per share}$$

*Municipal bond prices are typically quoted as a percent of par. A quote of 95 indicates that a bond is selling at 95 percent of its face value. A quote of 104 indicates a bond is selling for 104 percent of its face value. For example, a $5,000 principal amount municipal bond quoted at 104 has a market price of 104 percent of $5,000, or $5,200.

must liquidate a position in a fund may well find that the price received for the shares is less than the price that was paid for the shares.

The single most important variable that impacts the net asset values of municipal bond funds is interest rates. Rising interest rates drive down the market value of all bonds, including the tax-exempt securities held by municipal bond funds. Conversely, falling interest rates cause bond prices to rise and the net asset values of municipal bond funds to increase. As pointed out in Chapter 3, the longer a bond's maturity, the more the bond will change in price for a given change in interest rates. Thus, the net asset values of municipal bond funds that mostly hold long-term municipal bonds will experience greater variations for a given change in interest rates than will the net asset values of funds that mostly hold short- or medium-term municipal bonds.

Because the value of a mutual fund's shares fluctuates with the value of the securities that the fund holds, the selection of securities is very important. If the individuals who manage the fund's investments make superior decisions with respect to the securities that the fund holds, then the fund's stockholders will earn above-average returns. On the other hand, if the firm's managers do a poor job of selecting and managing the fund's securities, the fund's shares will perform poorly.

The municipal bond funds held by the fund and management's decisions about which bonds to buy and to sell will determine the return that a fund's shareholders will earn. A fund that restricts its portfolio to the very highest grade municipal bonds will pay shareholders a lower return, because high-grade municipal bonds tend to have lower yields than do lower-grade municipals that subject investors to greater risk. This doesn't mean that funds that own only high-grade municipal bonds are to be avoided, because these funds are likely to achieve above-average performance during periods of weak economic activity.

The Costs of Investing in Municipal Bond Funds

There are four potential expenses for investors in municipal bond funds. One of these costs applies in varying degrees to investors in any mutual fund. The other expenses are specific to individual funds and can be avoided if an investor is willing to do a little investigative work.

Every mutual fund incurs certain expenses; there are expenditures for a place to conduct business, salaries to pay the people who select the securities and handle the paperwork, and bills for utilities, to name just a few. The toll-free calls that shareholders make to a fund have to be paid for somewhere down the line. All of these expenses eventually must be paid by a fund's shareholders.

Mutual funds generally cover operating costs by assessing fees that are based on a percentage of the value of the assets owned by the fund. The annual management fee for most municipal bond funds will range from 1/2 of 1 percent to 1 percent of the fund's assets with the percentage declining as the value of the fund's assets increases (see Exhibit 6-3).

Exhibit 6-3
Calculation of a Municipal Bond Fund's
Annual Management Fee

The Town & City High-Yield Municipal Bond Fund has established the following schedule of annual management fees:

> 1.5% of the first $2,000,000 of fund assets
> 1.0% of the next $3,000,000 of fund assets
> .8% of the next $5,000,000 of fund assets
> .5% of all fund assets that exceed $10,000,000

With assets of $8,000,000, the fund's annual fee will be:

$$(.015)(\$2,000,000) + (.01)(\$3,000,000) + (.008)(\$3,000,000)$$
$$= \$30,000 + \$30,000 + \$24,000$$
$$= \$84,000$$

This fee represents $84,000/$8,000,000, or 1.05% of the value of the assets the fund holds.

With assets of $20,000,000, the fund's annual fee will be:

$$(.015)(\$2,000,000) + (.01)(\$3,000,000) + (.008)(\$5,000,000)$$
$$+ (.005)(\$10,000,000)$$

$$= \$30,000 + \$30,000 + \$40,000 + \$50,000$$
$$= \$150,000$$

The $150,000 fee represents $150,000/$20,000,000, or .75% of the fund's total assets.

Funds with a great amount of assets to manage will incur greater expenses than smaller funds although increases in expenses are not proportional to increases in assets. Thus, a fund with $200 million of assets to manage generally will levy a smaller proportional fee (but a larger dollar fee) than a fund with $50 million of assets to manage.

The amount of assets supervised by a fund is not the only consideration when municipal bond funds establish their management fees. Some funds make a determined effort to minimize operating expenses so that the funds' managers are able to levy fees proportionately smaller than those charged by competing funds of similar size. Fund managements attempt to keep expenses to a minimum not only as a good deed to the fund's shareholders, but because the individuals in charge realize that a lower fee results in higher yields that give the firm a competitive advantage when competing for investors' funds. Thus, a smaller percentage fee may result in sufficient additional investment funds so that management actually earns a greater dollar fee.

The expenses that municipal bond fund investors can avoid, at least to an extent, are the marketing or distribution fees that funds charge to shareholders. First, all mutual funds incur some distribution fees, and these fees must, in the end, be paid by the firm's stockholders. However, there are wide differences in the methods that funds utilize to promote and distribute their shares to the public and considerable differences in the distribution expenses that are incurred.

Distribution fees are levied for an entirely different purpose than managing the fund's portfolio of securities. Distribution fees are designed to cover the expenses of bringing new monies into a fund. Although aggressive marketing may cause the fund to grow and, thus, possibly result in a decrease in the proportional size of the management fee, distribution fees have little direct correlation with how a mutual fund performs and the return that is earned by the shareholders (except insofar as distribution fees reduce investor returns by increasing the cost of investing). Thus, it generally makes sense for investors to seek out funds that minimize distribution expenses.

There are several types of distribution fees that funds may charge their shareholders. The best-known of these fees is a front-end charge that is paid by investors at the time that shares are purchased. Called a *front-end load*, these charges constitute a percentage of the amount invested and range up to 6 percent for some municipal bond funds and up to 8 1/2 percent for some common stock funds. For example, an individual who invests $10,000 in a municipal bond fund that levies a 5 percent front-end load would find that only 95 percent of the amount invested actually is used to purchase shares of the fund because 5 percent is taken off the top as a sales charge. Front-end load fees are levied only once, at the time of purchase.

Front-end loads for mutual funds that levy such a fee generally range between 4 and 5 percent of the amount invested. Many funds levy a percentage sales fee that declines as the amount invested increases. Thus, an investor who purchases $50,000 of a municipal bond fund frequently will pay a lower percentage fee than an individual who invests only $5,000 in the same fund.

A different type of distribution charge involves a fee that is deducted from the proceeds when shares are redeemed. This type of charge, sometimes called a *rear-end load* or *exit fee*, is calculated as a

---

Exhibit 6-4
Typical Sales Charges on Municipal Bond Mutual Funds
with Front-End Loads

Amount of Investment	Sales Charge as Percent of Offering Price
Less than $25,000	5.00%
$25,000 to $99,000	4.00%
$100,000 to $249,999	3.25%
$250,000 to $499,999	2.50%
$500,000 to $999,999	2.00%
$1,000,000 to $1,999,999	1.00%
$2,000,000 to $4,999,999	0.50%
$5,000,000 and over	0.25%

percentage of the value of the shares being redeemed. Many of the mutual funds that have an exit charge set a percentage fee (of the value of the shares sold) that decreases the longer an investor has held the shares. For example, a mutual fund might quote a 6 percent exit fee that decreases by 1 percent each year during which shares in the fund are owned. Thus, an investor who holds shares in the fund for four years would have a 2 percent fee (6 percent reduced by 1 percent annually for four years) deducted from the value of redeemed shares.

The comparison of front-end loads and exit fees is not always as clear-cut as it may seem. For example, funds that levy exit fees frequently have slightly higher annual management fees. Thus, mutual funds with exit fees that decline with the length of the holding period are able to cover their distribution costs with an annual charge that many investors may overlook.

A third type of distribution charge that is paid by the owners of some municipal bond funds involves an annual fee levied against the firm's assets. As with management fees, the annual distribution charge is established as a percent of total assets managed by the fund. However, money collected from the distribution fee is used to support expenses incurred in selling shares of the fund rather than expenses involved in managing the portfolio. Mutual funds that levy a percentage fee against the assets they manage in order to support selling activities are designated as *12b-1 funds,* and the annual fees are known as *12b-1 fees.*

For funds that levy a separate sales or distribution charge, a 12b-1 fee is a smaller percentage of a fund's assets than either a front-end load or an exit fee. The problem is that the 12b-1 charge occurs each year that an investor owns a fund so that over a long period of time the recurring annual fee will likely turn out to be significantly larger than either of the other sales fees. For the short-term investor, the 12b-1 fee is not as significant because the charge will only be paid a few times.

Summarizing Municipal Bond Funds

The major advantages offered by a municipal bond fund are instant diversification, professional management of a municipal bond

---

Exhibit 6-5
Pay Now or Pay Later—Does It Matter?

The Jack Greenhill Low-Risk Municipal Bond Fund has a one-time front-end load fee that is equal to 5 percent of the amount an individual invests. The virtually identical Saterbo AAA-Rated Municipal Bond Fund has no front-end load, but management has established an exit fee of 5 percent. The Saterbo fee does not decline for longer holding periods. If both funds produce the same yields, does it matter which fund an investor purchases?

If $10,000 is invested in the front-end Jack Greenhill Fund, the investor's $10,000 investment will be reduced by a $500 sales fee (5 percent of $10,000), with the result that $9,500 worth of shares will be acquired. Assuming that the shares increase in value at an annual rate of 3 percent, the investor's stake will have risen to a value of $12,767 by the end of ten years. This terminal value of $12,767 does not account for any interest distributions to owners of the fund and does not assume any reinvestment on the part of the investor.

If $10,000 is invested in the Saterbo Fund, the full amount of the investment will go toward the purchase of the fund's shares. Assuming that the Saterbo Fund also increases in value at a rate of 3 percent annually, the initial $10,000 investment will have grown to attain a market value of $13,439 in ten years. However, the investor in the Saterbo Fund still is obligated to pay the 5 percent exit fee at the time that the fund's shares are sold. If the shares are liquidated at the end of ten years, the investor will recover $13,439 less the 5 percent fee of $672, or $12,767. Thus, the investor comes out with the same amount of money regardless of whether the sales fee is charged on the front-end or at the time the shares are redeemed.

One consideration for investors who purchase shares in municipal bond funds is that a major part of the return will come from tax-exempt interest payments that are passed through to shareholders. Larger interest payments will result if the distribution fee is in the form of an exit charge because all of the initial investment goes into purchasing shares of the fund. In the above case, the investor would have the full $10,000 purchase price invested in interest-earning assets.

portfolio, and an incremental investment requirement that is significantly smaller than is required to purchase individual municipal bonds. Unfortunately, these benefits are not without a cost. All municipal bond funds charge investors an annual management fee that can reduce the annual rate of return by up to 1 percent. If sales fees are added on top of a management fee, the reduction in yield can be substantial.

Investors with substantial funds who have access to knowledgeable brokers at firms that provide adequate resources are likely to

---

Exhibit 6-6
The Whys and Why Nots of Municipal Bond Funds

Why Buy Municipal Bond Funds

- They offer an already diversified portfolio of municipal bonds.
- Professionals select the bonds and manage the portfolio.
- It requires a relatively small investment compared to purchasing individual issues of municipal bonds.
- Worries about calls, interest payments, etc. are taken care of by the fund.
- It is relatively easy to liquidate shares.
- It is easy to keep track of the value.

Why Not Buy Municipal Bond Funds

- Annual management fee may reduce annual yield by up to 1 percent.
- Many funds charge a separate distribution fee.
- It's not as possible to tailor a portfolio to personal needs as when individual bonds are selected.
- It is difficult to avoid state and local taxation.
- Investors lack control over the selection of bonds.
- The potential exists for an investor to be surprised by relatively risky bonds owned by the fund.

be best served by putting together their own diversified portfolio of municipal bonds. Purchasing individual bonds allows an investor to avoid the expenses involved in buying and owning shares of a mutual fund and allows an investor to select bonds that best fit his or her own needs. On the other hand, investors of modest means likely will find that the charges levied by municipal bond funds are a reasonable cost for the benefits that these funds offer.

MUNICIPAL BOND TRUSTS

Investors who seek a ready-made portfolio of municipal bonds have an avenue other than municipal bond mutual funds. Municipal bond trusts (sometimes called *unit trusts* or *unit investment trusts*) offer the same basic benefits as municipal bond mutual funds, but the trusts produce these benefits using a slightly different financial structure that alters the fees that investors face.

The Structure of Municipal Bond Trusts

A municipal bond trust consists of a pool of municipal bonds of which ownership components called *units* are sold to investors. Sponsors of a trust assemble the municipal bonds that are to be included in the trust and then sell a fixed number of trust units to investors. The price at which the units are sold depends upon the value of the bonds in the trust and the number of units issued. Except for redemptions at maturity or through calls, the pool of municipal bonds within a trust remains unchanged and unmanaged during the life of the trust. A newly-organized trust might contain fourteen or fifteen different municipal bond issues with a total principal of $10 million and have 10,000 ownership units outstanding. Although all the bonds will not necessarily be valued at par, the units of ownership will have a value of approximately $1,000 ($10,000,000/10,000 units).

Municipal bond trusts can consist of geographically diversified portfolios of tax-exempt bonds or a more narrowly defined group of bonds that appeal to investors in need of a specialized portfolio. For example, some trusts are formed with only intermediate-length bonds that attract investors who desire a relatively early return of their principal or who are concerned by the changing values that accompany bonds with long maturities. Other trusts appeal to risk-adverse investors by investing only in bonds at or above a certain rating or bonds that are insured.

To appeal to investors in states with high state income tax rates, sponsors sometimes form trusts that own only bonds issued within a particular state. Thus, these trusts make payments that are free from state (depending upon state laws) as well as federal taxation. For such a strategy to be financially viable for sponsors, single state municipal bond trusts are pretty much limited to states that have fairly high tax rates and substantial populations.

The lack of portfolio management in a trust differs greatly from municipal bond mutual funds where portfolio managers continually buy and sell securities in an attempt to increase the yield and upgrade the quality of the funds' portfolios. A mutual fund is a continuing, on-going financial organization that has no scheduled termination date. That is, there is no specific date when the owners are scheduled to have their shares redeemed and their monies returned. A trust, however, will be liquidated gradually.

A municipal bond trust is organized so that, as bonds held by the trust are redeemed by their respective issuers at maturity or through calls, owners of the trust have portions of their principal returned. At some point, all of the bonds that initially were acquired to form the trust will have been redeemed so that no assets will remain, and the trust will no longer exist. Sponsors continually bring new trusts to market as investor demand warrants.

Although both mutual funds and trusts provide investors with diversified portfolios or professionally selected municipal bonds, a trust has no further need for management once the portfolio of bonds has been assembled, and the units of ownership have been distributed to investors. None of the bonds in the portfolio will be sold (except in very unusual circumstances), and no additional bonds will be purchased.

The Value of Tax-Exempt Trust Units

Municipal trust units are valued in the same manner as shares of municipal bond mutual funds. That is, the value of a trust unit is equal to the market value of all the bonds owned by a trust divided by the number of units of trust ownership that are outstanding. As the market values of bonds within a trust change, the values of shares of ownership of the trust change. If for some reason one of the issuers of bonds held by a trust defaults, the value of those bonds in all probability will decline substantially in market value.

Municipal bond values are driven primarily by interest rates so that the values of municipal bond trust units fluctuate with changes in interest rates. Rising market rates of interest depress the market values of the municipal bonds held by a trust and, thus, decrease the value of the ownership units of the trust. Falling market rates of interest provide an upward boost to trust unit values. If the coupons of the bonds contained in a trust are lower than the going rate of interest on bonds of similar risk and maturity, the trust units must sell at a discount from the price that would exist of all of the bonds in the trust sold at par. Conversely, if the bonds contained in a trust have high coupon rates compared to the coupons on newly issued bonds, the trust units will sell at a premium to the price that would exist if all of the bonds in the trust sold at par.

A trust's current yield (annual interest paid per unit divided by the unit price) is dependent upon the coupons of the individual municipal bonds held in the trust. The current yield will be quite high if a trust is holding a substantial number of high-coupon bonds even though these securities may suddenly decrease in value as bonds are called or as the bonds decline in price toward par value at maturity (see Exhibit 6-7). In either instance an investor who buys into the trust is gaining current yield at the expense of future capital losses. This practice is no different than when an investor buys individual issues of high-coupon municipal bonds, but trusts frequently are purchased by investors who fail to examine the details of individual bonds in the trust's portfolio.

Investors in tax-exempt trusts cannot redeem units of ownership in the same manner as owners of mutual fund shares. The sponsor of a trust generally is not required to repurchase units that have been sold to investors although most sponsors maintain a secondary market in units of the trusts that they originate. Repurchased units are offered for resale to other investors. Sponsors make these secondary markets both to provide liquidity to owners of trusts

---

Exhibit 6-7
Example of a Municipal Bond Trust
Containing High-Coupon Bonds

Bond	Principal Amount	Price*	Value
City of Scully, CA 12s00	$ 300,000	116.22	$ 348,660
Beard Water Works 12s05	250,000	127.18	317,950
Holland County Housing 10s00	400,000	108.11	432,440
Woelfel County, SD, Jail 14s05	300,000	140.77	422,310
Mt l, IN Housing Project 12s00	500,000	116.22	581,100
Roger's Rock Museum 14s00	250,000	124.43	311,080
Total	$2,000,000		$2,413,540

*Prices assume that individual bonds sell to yield 8 percent at their respective maturities.

If there are 100,000 units of the trust, each unit should sell for approximately $2,413,540/100,000, or $24.14. The current yield will be the annual interest that is paid per trust unit ($243,000/100,000 units = $2.43) divided by the unit price ($24.14), or 10.1 percent.

Thus, the trust units offer a very high current yield that can mislead investors who do not realize that bonds held by the trust will suffer substantial losses in market value as the securities approach maturity. Losses in market value will offset a portion of current interest payments to produce an overall annual yield of 8 percent. If any of the bonds are called prior to maturity, the yield to the investor will be even lower than 8 percent.

(which, in turn, makes the trusts initially easier to sell) and to produce a profit for themselves.

Investors who decide to sell trust units back to the sponsor generally will receive a price that is based upon the bid prices of the bonds held by the trust. That is, the price paid by the sponsor to repurchase trust units from investors is dependent upon the prices that individual bonds in the trust would bring if these bonds were sold in the secondary market. Because of the potential conflict of interest if the sponsor of the trust determined the value of the trust's units in the secondary market, an independent evaluator prices the bonds. The difference between the bid and ask prices of municipal bonds in the secondary market can sometimes be several points so that the price received from selling units of a municipal bond trust may be less than an investor expects. Differences between the bid and ask prices are moderated by the bids being calculated on the basis of the large numbers of bonds within the trusts' portfolios.

Costs of Investing in Municipal Bond Trusts

The major cost of investing in a municipal bond trust is the sales fee that must be paid at the time the units are purchased. These sales fees, generally ranging between 2 percent and 5 percent of the amount invested, are added to the investor's purchase. Thus, an individual investing $5,000 in a trust that charges a 4 percent sales fee will have an additional $200 (.04 times $5,000) added to the purchase price. The percentage fee is determined by the trust's sponsor. Fees tend to be at the high end of the 2 to 5 percent range on long-term trusts (trusts containing long-term bonds) and at the low end of the range on short-term trusts.

Sales fees for investment trusts frequently vary with the amount of money that an individual invests. To attract investors with large amounts of money, sponsors may establish a fee schedule in which the percentage charge declines as the amount of money invested increases. For most investors, fees for purchasing unit trusts in the primary market tend to range between 3 1/2 to 4 1/2 percent of the amount invested.

When an investor purchases trust units in the secondary market (units that a sponsor has repurchased from another investor and then offered for resale), the new buyer will be required to pay a sales fee that may either be the same or slightly different than the percentage fee that was charged during the initial offering of the units. For example, a sponsor that charges a 4 1/2 percent fee on an initial offering might charge a fee of 5 1/2 percent on units that are sold in the secondary market.

A sponsor may charge an investor who purchases trust units in the secondary market a price based either on the bid prices or the offering prices of the bonds contained in the trust. If bid prices are used, the sponsor generally imposes a higher percentage sales fee. As is the case with unit trusts sold in the primary market, the percentage fee on sales of trust units in the secondary market often declines as the amount invested increases. A typical fee schedule for the sponsor of a municipal bond unit trust is displayed in Exhibit 6-8. The first schedule applies to trust units initially offered to the public, and the second schedule is applicable to units that have been repurchased by the sponsor and are being reoffered in the secondary market.

Summarizing Municipal Bond Trusts

Municipal trusts offer investors adequate diversification at what is generally a reasonable cost. The trust sponsor puts together a portfolio of municipal bonds, sells units of ownership in the portfolio to investors, and then passes on interest and principal payments to the owners. New bonds are not purchased so that the trust is not

---

Exhibit 6-8
Typical Municipal Trust Sales Fees

	Sales Charge as Percentage of Offering Price	
Number of Units	Initial Offering	Secondary Market*
Less than 250	4.5%	5.5%
250 to 499	3.5%	4.5%
500 to 749	3.0%	3.5%
750 to 999	2.5%	2.5%
1,000 or more	2.0%	2.0%

*On reoffered units the percentage is based on the bid side of bonds included in the trust.

---

on-going. At some point, all of the bonds in a trust will have been redeemed by the borrowers and the trust will cease to exist.

Trusts appeal primarily to investors who are looking at municipal bonds on a long-term or intermediate-term basis (as opposed to a trading basis) and who either don't have sufficient funds to acquire a diversified portfolio of bonds or who just don't feel comfortable putting together a municipal bond portfolio on their own. For either of these investors, the purchase of municipal bond trusts is a good method of acquiring tax-exempt income.

Exhibit 6-9
The Whys and Why Nots of Municipal Bond Trusts

Why Buy Municipal Bond Trusts

- They offer an already diversified portfolio of bonds.
- Municipal bonds are selected professionally.
- The investment required is small compared to that required for individual issues of municipal bonds.
- Investors need not worry about individual interest payments or redemptions—these are taken care of by the trust sponsor.
- It is relatively easy to dispose of units.
- No annual management fee is assessed as it is with municipal bond mutual funds.

Why Not Buy Municipal Bond Trusts

- They charge front-end sales fees of between 3 and 5 percent of the amount invested, which reduces yields.
- The investor may encounter difficulty in locating trusts that provide payments exempt from state and local taxation.
- It is very difficult to calculate a unit's yield to maturity.
- Risky bonds can be hidden in a trust portfolio.
- A large investment is required compared to that required by municipal bond mutual funds.

Unless there is a reasonable possibility that an investor will have to liquidate an investment position within several years, trusts generally offer a lower-cost option for acquiring municipal bonds than do mutual funds that specialize in municipal bonds. The reason is that mutual funds levy annual management fees that range from 1/2 to 1 percent while trusts remain unmanaged once the portfolio has been put together.

Individuals with fairly large sums of money for investment are likely to earn greater yields by purchasing individual issues of municipal bonds, because there will be no management or sales fees. However, unless an investor has an adequate understanding of municipal bonds or the assistance of someone who does, a real possibility for tragedy exists. Choosing among the multitude of issuers, maturities, and yields to put together a portfolio of municipal bonds takes more than guesswork. Overpaying for bonds in the secondary market can easily wipe away any money saved by avoiding the sales fee levied by a trust's sponsor.

Appendix A

MUNICIPAL BOND RATINGS

Bond ratings represent the analysis and subsequent grading of fixed income securities by professional security analysts. The two largest and best known agencies that rate fixed income securities are Standard and Poor's and Moody's. Two additional rating agencies are Fitch Investors Service and Duff and Phelps. Rating agencies grade the investment quality of many municipal bond issues as well as a large number of corporate securities and then make the quality ratings available to both individual and institutional investors.

In grading municipal securities, the rating agencies perform a fundamental analysis of both issuers and individual issues, thus saving investors from performing this task themselves. Individual investors rely heavily on published ratings of the agencies so the rating assigned to a particular issue has a major impact upon the interest rate that must be paid to investors in order to sell the debt issue. Receiving a higher rating on a large debt issue can save a municipality millions of dollars in interest expenses over the life of an issue.

Most investors consider a bond's rating to be so important that new municipal bond issues may be relatively difficult to market if they do not have the independent gradings. Thus, a municipality wishing to issue debt is often willing to pay one or more of the rating agencies thousands of dollars to have the securities rated. A rating also makes it easier for an investor to resell a municipal bond in the secondary market.

Municipal bond analysis is very comprehensive and revolves around the ability of a municipality (in the case of a general obligation issue) or a municipal project (in the case of a revenue bond) to adequately service an issue of debt over the issue's lifetime. Among other variables considered in establishing ratings are economic forecasts, financial resources of the issuer, specific terms of an issue, credit supports such as insurance or a letter of credit, existing debt and other financial obligations of the issuer, and the quality of a municipality's or a municipal project's administrators.

Rating agencies will alter the rating of an issue after the issue has been sold if the ability of the issuer to service this debt changes significantly. Thus, municipal bonds may be downgraded or upgraded by the agencies following events such as a substantial change in a community's economic base (e.g., a large employer leaves the community) or a major decline in a community's indebtedness.

Rating categories of the two major rating agencies are illustrated in Exhibit A-1. The grades and categories are virtually identical for both rating firms and individual security issues generally are rated the same by both organizations. However, in some cases an issue may have a split rating, meaning that the two firms view an issue differently. For example, Standard and Poor's may assign a rating of AA while Moody's grades the same issue as an A. In other instances an issue may be rated by only a single agency.

Standard and Poor's uses plus (+) and minus (-) symbols to indicate relative differences within a rating category while Moody's uses the numbers 1, 2, and 3 for the same purposes. For example, ratings of BBB+ and Baa1 both indicate issues that are judged to be at the high end of this lower investment-grade category. A rating of at least BBB (S&P) or Baa (Moody's) is necessary for an issue to be considered investment grade.

Exhibit A-1
Municipal Bond Ratings

Moody's	S&P	
Aaa	AAA	High-grade with extremely strong capacity to pay principal and interest.
Aa	AA	High-grade by all standards but with slightly lower margins of protection than AAA.
A	A	Medium-grade with favorable investment attributes but with some susceptibility to adverse economic changes.
Baa	BBB	Medium-grade with adequate capacity to pay interest and principal but possibly lacking certain protection against adverse economic conditions.
Ba	BB	Speculative with moderate protection of principal and interest in an unstable economy.
B	B	Speculative and lacking desirable characteristics of investment bonds. Small assurance of principal and interest.
Caa	CCC	Issue in default or in danger of default.
Ca	CC	Highly speculative and in default or with other market shortcomings.
C		Extremely poor investment quality.
	C	Income bonds paying no interest.
D		In default with interest or principal in arrears.

Appendix B

HISTORICAL YIELDS ON MUNICIPAL AND CORPORATE BONDS

Exhibit B-1
Tax-Exempt and Taxable Interest Rates

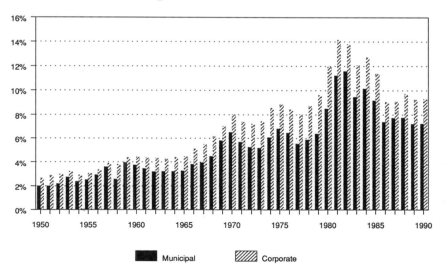

Appendix C

STATE TAXATION OF MUNICIPAL BONDS

Most states that tax income require that residents include any interest from municipal bonds issued by other states but not interest from municipal bonds issued within that state. Thus, a resident of California must pay California income taxes on the interest received from a bond issued by the state of Indiana, but the resident does not have to pay this same California tax on interest received from a tax-exempt bond issued by the city of San Francisco. There are exceptions, and some states tax all municipal income while other states exempt all municipal income from taxation. Of course, a few states still have no income tax at the state level.

States that tax income generally require that investors include as income a realized capital gain on any municipal bond. For example, Indiana levies no income tax against any municipal bond interest but does levy the tax against gains that are realized when municipal bonds that are sold or redeemed at a profit.

States with an intangible tax generally levy the tax against the market values of municipal bonds issued by other states but do not levy an intangible tax against the market values of municipal bonds issued within that state. As with the case of income taxation, there are exceptions to this rule.

Most bonds issued by Guam, Puerto Rico, and the Virgin Islands are exempt from any taxation by any state. Thus, a resident of New York can avoid the New York income tax on interest income received from a bond issued by Puerto Rico.

Exhibit C-1 illustrates taxation of municipal bonds at the state level. Keep in mind that taxation at the state level is in constant flux (in a mostly upward direction). Be certain to double-check the tax code currently in effect rather than rely solely on the data of Exhibit C-1.

Exhibit C-1
State Taxation of Municipal Bonds

	Income Tax on Interest	Intangible Tax
Alabama	O	O
Alaska	N	N
Arizona	O	N
Arkansas	O	B
California	O	N
Colorado	O	N
Connecticut	N	N
Delaware	O	N
District of Columbia	O	N
Florida	N	O
Georgia	O	O
Hawaii	O	N
Idaho	O	B
Illinois	B	N
Indiana	N	N
Iowa	B	N
Kansas	B	O
Kentucky	O	O
Louisiana	O	O
Maine	O	N
Maryland	O	N
Massachusetts	O	N
Michigan	O	O
Minnesota	O	N
Mississippi	O	N
Missouri	O	N
Montana	O	B
Nebraska	N	N
Nevada	N	N
New Hampshire	O	N

Exhibit continues

Exhibit C-1
State Taxation of Municipal Bonds (Continued)

	Income Tax On Interest	Intangible Tax
New Jersey	O	N
New Mexico	N	N
New York	O	N
North Carolina	O	O
North Dakota	O	N
Ohio	O	B
Oklahoma	B	N
Oregon	O	N
Pennsylvania	O	O
Rhode Island	O	N
South Carolina	O	N
South Dakota	N	O
Tennessee	O	N
Texas	N	N
Utah	N	N
Vermont	O	N
Virginia	O	N
Washington	N	N
West Virginia	O	O
Wisconsin	B	N
Wyoming	N	N

B = Both in-state and out-of-state bonds
N = Neither in-state nor out-of-state bonds
O = Out-of-state bonds only

APPENDIX D

THE ALTERNATIVE MINIMUM TAX AND MUNICIPAL BONDS

by Donald Seat

The alternative minimum tax (AMT) originated with the Tax Reform Act of 1969. The impetus for an AMT was the public disclosure that many wealthy individuals and businesses were manipulating the tax laws to their advantage and avoiding any liability for federal income taxes. One of the examples of legal tax avoidance presented to Congress involved a widow who paid no income taxes despite the fact that she received several million dollars of annual income from municipal bond interest. Public sentiment was strong that anyone with such a large amount of income should pay income taxes.

Congress proceeded to pass an AMT law that subjected many tax-advantaged situations to taxation. Ironically, interest from tax-exempt securities was not considered subject to AMT rules until the Tax Reform Act of 1986 was passed nearly two decades later.

The Tax Reform Act of 1986 subjects the interest from *private activity bonds* to the alternative minimum tax. Section 141 of the

Internal Revenue Code defines a municipal bond as being in the private category if:

1. more than 10 percent of the issue's proceeds is to be used for any private business;

2. payment of principal or interest on more than 10 percent of the issue (directly or indirectly) is secured by any interest in property that is used or is to be used for a private business or for payments in respect of such property; or the proceeds of the issue are to be derived from payments with respect to property or borrowed money that is used or to be used for private business; and

3. proceeds of the issue are used to make or finance loans to persons other than governmental units and these loans exceed the lesser of five percent of the proceeds or $5 million.

Another section of the Code specifies that, for alternative minimum tax purposes, interest will be subject to preference rules if private activity bonds were issued after August 7, 1986, and the interest is not includable in gross income under section 103. If the bonds are issued to refund bonds issued prior to August 8, 1986, the securities will not be included in the AMT calculation.

Also, bonds issued by defined tax exempt organizations and governmental agencies are exempted from private activity bonds status. A $150 million cap is placed on issues from tax exempt organizations other than hospitals.

The greatest difficulty with regard to interest on private activity bonds is definitional. That is, it may be difficult to determine if a specific bond issue meets the requirements of the IRS Code and is exempt from the alternative minimum tax. There also exists the possibility that the purchaser of a bond may be misled (usually unintentionally) by the issuing agency to believe that the bond proceeds will be used entirely for public purposes. If the proceeds are then utilized for other purposes and the "10 percent rule" violated, interest from the bonds may be subject to the alternative minimum tax.

If an investor discovers that interest income is subject to the AMT, any interest expense that is incurred in carrying the bonds (and that is disallowed as a deduction for regular tax purposes) is deductible before including the amount in alternative minimum taxable income.

Tax preferences for AMT purposes are classified into the following categories:

1. Depletion—the amount deducted in the current year in excess of the property's adjusted basis.

2. Intangible drilling cost—the amount by which the excess intangible drilling costs arising during the year exceed 65 percent of the taxpayer's income from oil, gas, and geothermal properties.

3. Bad debt losses of financial institutions—the amount in excess of the actual writeoffs that is classified as a reserve. This preference is not applicable to individual investors.

4. Tax-exempt interest—interest on *private activity bonds* reduced by any deductions that would have been allowable if such interest was includable in gross income.

5. Appreciated property charitable contribution—the excess charitable contribution taken over the adjusted basis of contributed property.

6. Accelerated depreciation on pre-1987 property—the excess of accelerated depreciation over straight-line depreciation.

In general, the category of adjustments relates to "timing differences" between book income and tax income. Depreciation is an excellent example. To the extent that the depreciation claimed exceeds straight line depreciation, the difference is a positive adjustment (i.e. it increases the alternative minimum taxable income). When this situation reverses, a negative adjustment occurs, and the AMT is reduced.

An exemption is allowed in computations for the alternative minimum tax. For single individuals, the exemption is $30,000; for mar-

Exhibit D-1
Basic Formula for Calculating the Alternative Minimum Tax

Regular taxable income from Form 1040	$ XXXX
Add: Tax preferences	+ XX
Positive "adjustments"	+ XX
Deduct: Negative "adjustments"	–XX
Alternative minimum taxable income	$ XXXXX
Less: Exemption	–XXX
Tax base	$XXXXX
Multiply by AMT tax rate	.21
AMT before foreign tax credit	$ XXX
Less: Foreign tax credit	–XX
Tentative alternative minimum tax	$ XXX
Less: Regular tax (from Form 1040)	–XX
Alternative Minimum Tax (if positive)	$ XX

If negative, the AMT does not apply for the year, and the taxpayer's liability is the regular tax indicated on Form 1040.

---

ried couples filing a joint return the exemption is $40,000, and for married couples filing separate returns the exemption is $20,000 each.

Donald Seat, CPA, holds a Ph.D. in accounting from the University of Kentucky and is Chairman of the Accounting and Finance Department at Valdosta State College.

Appendix E

HOW MUNICIPAL BONDS COME TO MARKET

by Stephanie G. Bigwood

Municipal bonds are brought to market either on a competitive or negotiated basis. In either case, the ideas for the bond issue begin with a decision on the part of the municipality that a large amount of financing is required for some particular purpose, i.e. the construction of a new library. After much study and public debate, there generally will be a vote of the citizens who will be affected, thus giving those who are being asked to pay for financing the facility the opportunity to say yes or no. A public referendum frequently is required because an increase in taxes may be necessary to provide the monies needed to retire the new bond issue. In some cases in which bonds are serviced by revenues from a project the borrowed funds are used to finance, no public referendum is required.

After voter approval (if required) has been obtained, municipal officers will meet with bond advisors from various investment banking firms and/or commercial banks, as well as with bond counsel. One decision is when to "come to market," that is to say, when the municipality will issue the bonds. It also will be necessary to design the structure of the offering and have bond counsel review the plan to make certain that the issue is being legally designed and properly described in the Preliminary Official Statement that must be made available to the investing public. The bond counsel also must pass judgment with regard to the bonds' qualification for the tax status (tax-exempt, subject to or exempt from AMT, or taxable with respect to federal income taxes) as it is to be described in the Preliminary Official Statement.

Most general obligation bond issues utilize a competitive offering in which many different underwriting groups are invited to bid for the opportunity to market the entire issue. Each underwriting group, also called a *syndicate*, consists of one or more investment banking firms or commercial banks that will manage the group, as well as several other similar firms that will assist in the offering. Although these firms are competitors in soliciting business from individual and institutional investors, investment banking firms and commercial banks frequently join forces to bring a new security issue to market. In acting together, the firms are able to underwrite and share the risk in selling large security issues. Otherwise, any given firm acting alone would be severely limited in the amount of any one security issue it could underwrite because a mistake in judgment could significantly impair that firm's capital.

Firms that are not part of the underwriting group may be allowed to participate in the sale of the new issue; collectively they make up what is called the *selling group*. Members of the selling group typically will not be allowed to earn the same profit on the sale of a new bond during the time the bond remains in the syndicate, but members at least have the opportunity to fill client orders to buy the bonds being offered.

Sealed bids that fall within the confines of certain prepublished standards will be accepted on a predetermined date at a pre-announced hour (typically 11 a.m. or noon) by a representative of the municipality that is issuing the bonds. All bids are then reviewed while representatives of the various underwriting group await word as to which group "won" the bonds. The bid submitted by the underwriting group that is willing to pay the highest price for the bond issue, and thereby raise the funds at the lowest net interest cost to the municipality, will be awarded the bond issue. The winning group will buy the entire bond issue and then resell the securities to the investing public at whatever price the syndicate

can obtain. The difference between the price paid to the municipality and the price at which the bonds are reoffered to the public
represents the spread or profit per bond that the underwriting
group will earn.

Should conditions change in the bond market before all of the
securities are placed with investors, the underwriting group may
lower the reoffering price for bonds that remain in the syndicate. It
also is possible that changing market conditions prior to the bond
issue being completely sold out might cause the underwriters to
consider raising the price at which they will reoffer the remaining
bonds. If the underwriters choose to raise the reoffering price of the
bonds, they typically will declare that the issue is freed from syndicate so that syndicate members will be free to trade the bonds at
any price they wish. In some instances, the underwriters will
choose to leave the bonds in syndicate even though market conditions have improved.

While bonds remain in syndicate, no syndicate member is permitted to undercut the established reoffering price, and generally
bonds are not reoffered at a price above that set by the syndicate. To
charge a higher price would make the bonds less attractive than the
issue's description in the final version of the Official Statement that
accompanies every confirmation that bond dealers send to clients
who bought the original bonds. The terms of the new issue also will
be advertised in leading financial publications such as *The Wall
Street Journal* and *The Daily Bond Buyer* if the issue is of any size, and
the issue will certainly be advertised in newspapers in the community where the bonds are being issued.

Some municipal bond issues, especially revenue bond issues, are
brought to market on a negotiated, as opposed to a competitive,
basis. Negotiated deals are brought to market by investment banking firms and/or commercial banks that have worked with the issuing municipality to set the details of the offering. The municipality
may make known in advance that it will be bringing out the bond
issue, but it does not announce in advance the date and time of the
offering. Rather, the issuer works with the underwriters to determine the correct timing, given conditions in the marketplace and
the level of advance interest the underwriters have been able to
generate for the planned issue. Bonds sometimes are priced and

offered for resale to the investing public shortly after some favorable economic news has improved conditions in the bond market.

One major distinction between competitive and negotiated municipal bond issues is the risk assumed by the underwriting group. In most competitive offerings, the underwriters are liable for the entire bond issue as the issue originally has been priced regardless of whether the market demand for the issue turns out to be as strong as anticipated. Thus, if fewer investors have an interest in the bonds than was anticipated, the syndicate may have to reduce the reoffering price and either accept less profit, or possibly take a loss on the remaining bonds.

The price for a negotiated bond offering is not final until the underwriters announce that it is final. Thus, if the underwriting group overestimates the demand for a bond issue at a particular yield, the group can notify all buyers and potential buyers that it will again take orders at a higher yield (e.g., a lower price) for a limited time. Buyers who previously committed to invest will be given the higher yield, and investors who were considering the bonds but did not place orders, hopefully will become interested at the higher yield. It is possible, but unlikely, that the bonds will be repriced again, as most underwriters have expertise in judging the price concessions that are required to sell new issues.

A negotiated bond offering can be repriced at a lower yield (or higher price) in the event that an offering is substantially oversubscribed at the original yield. In this event, the investors who previously agreed to purchase the bonds at the announced yields will be contacted by their brokers and informed of the new reoffering yields and prices. Investors are not held to their initial orders and are given preferential treatment in purchasing bonds at the reduced yields. While further yield and price adjustments might occur, the bonds usually need only one repricing to obtain the correct balance between the supply and demand.

After the underwriters determine that the balance is sufficiently close for the offering to be successful and the bond issuer has agreed to the new terms, the manager of the underwriting group will allocate the bonds among the various firms participating in the offering. These firms, in turn, will place the allocated bonds with clients who have entered orders. At this time, perhaps hours or even a day or two after the bond seller took the client's original order, the seller finally confirms to the client that the order was filled at the agreed yield and price.

The negotiated bond offering is aptly named. Although it may take a bit longer to complete a purchase transaction for a negotiated bond issue in the primary market, both the underwriting group and the investing public are assured that the yield at which the bond is brought to market is a fair representation of existing market conditions. It is possible to buy a competitively priced bond in the primary market only to learn at the end of the day that the issue has not sold well and that 80 percent of the issue remains in the syndicate; in this case, price cuts on remaining bonds are likely in the next day or two unless market conditions improve.

Stephanie Bigwood has worked as a bond trader and as a broker at both the institutional and retail level. She is currently a treasury officer at Maryland National Bank.

Appendix F

GLOSSARY

above par Pertaining to a bond that sells for more than par value.

accretion The accumulation of gains on discount bonds. The accreted value of a municipal bond gradually increases from the bond's issue price to the bond's maturity value.

accrued interest Interest that is owed but not yet paid. Because interest on most municipal bonds is paid semi-annually, an investor who purchases municipal bonds in the secondary market must pay the seller interest that has accrued on the bond since the last interest payment date.

ad valorem tax A tax that is levied against the market value of a specific property. An example is the intangible tax local governments sometimes levy against the market value of municipal bonds.

alternative minimum tax (AMT) A federal tax levied against taxable income as adjusted for specific items such as the interest from certain municipal bonds. The alternative minimum tax is paid by few individuals and is generally applicable to individuals who have substantial income that is sheltered from taxation.

American Municipal Bond Assurance Corporation (AMBAC) A private insurance company that insures interest and principal payments on municipal bonds. Municipalities buy the insurance in order to reduce the interest rate that must be paid to sell municipal bonds to the public.

arbitrage bond A municipal bond that is issued so that the issuer can invest the proceeds in securities that provide yields higher than the yield paid on the municipal bond.

basis point One one-hundredth of one percent. Yield differences among bonds are measured in basis points.

bearer bond A bond with no owner's name on the certificate and no name registered with the issuer. New issues of municipal bonds in bearer form were prohibited beginning in 1983.

below par Pertaining to a security that sells at less than the security's par value.

Blue List A daily Standard & Poor's publication that contains offerings of municipal bonds.

bond anticipation note A short-term municipal security requiring that repayment be made from the proceeds of a long-term issue of bonds that will be sold at a later date.

bond bank A bond pool organized and sponsored by a state.

Bond Buyer's Index An index of municipal bond yields that is published by *The Bond Buyer*.

bond pool A municipal bond of a number of cities or tax-exempt organizations that would be unable to issue bonds on their own because of their small size.

bond rating A quality grading of municipal debt that measures the issuer's ability to meet interest and principal requirements in a timely manner. Ratings range from AAA (the highest rating) to C (the lowest rating).

bond swap Selling a bond at the same time as purchasing one. Most swaps of municipal bonds are undertaken in order to produce a loss for tax purposes.

call price The price at which an issuer may redeem a security prior to the security's scheduled maturity. Calls can be made at par value or at a premium to par value depending upon the details contained in a bond's offering statement.

call protection A prohibition against an issuer calling a security during a prescribed period following the date of issue. For long-term municipal bonds, the period of call protection is generally ten years.

competitive bidding The process by which an organization desiring to raise funds in the capital markets selects an investment banker on the basis of the price offered for securities that are to be issued. In the case of a proposed issue of municipal bonds, competitive bidding would result in the issuer accepting the highest price (lowest interest cost) for the proposed issue.

coupon The annual interest payment on a security. A municipal security pays annual interest equal to the bond's coupon times the principal amount. For example, a $5,000 principal amount municipal bond with an eight percent coupon will pay an investor $400 annually.

coupon bond *See* bearer bond.

current yield The annual rate of return from a municipal bond based upon the annual interest payment and the current price at which the bond sells. Current yield may misrepresent the overall return that will be earned from owning a security.

dated date The date on which a newly issued bond begins accruing interest.

dealer A firm or an individual that buys securities for and sells assets from its own portfolio.

debt service The amount of funds required to meet interest, principal, and sinking fund requirements during a given period of time.

default Failure of a borrower to live up to the terms of a contract.

defeasance Extinguishing an existing debt by presenting the trustee with a portfolio of securities sufficient to take care of the requirements of the existing debt.

denomination The face value of a security. Most municipal bonds are denominated in units of $5,000.

discount bond A bond that sells for less than the bond's face value.

double-barreled municipal bond A municipal bond that is secured by a particular revenue source as well as by the general obligation of the issuer.

double-exempt fund An investment company that limits its investments to municipal bonds of a single state so that interest paid by the bonds and passed through by the fund is exempt from both federal and state taxation.

equivalent taxable yield The taxable return that must be earned to equal, on an aftertax basis, the return that is available on a tax-exempt investment.

essential function bond A municipal bond in which the funds that are raised are utilized for traditional government purposes such as building schools and roads.

first call date The earliest date that an issuer can call bonds of a particular issue.

first coupon date The date on which a bond makes the initial interest payment.

501(c)(3) bond A bond issued by a nonprofit hospital or college that pays interest that is tax-exempt and that is not subject to the alternative minimum tax.

flat scale A municipal bond offering in which yields are approximately the same at all maturities.

full-faith-and-credit pledge A municipality's pledge that all of the financial resources and taxing power of the municipality are behind a bond issue.

general obligation bond Municipal debt for which the full financial resources and taxing power of the issuer secure the interest and principal.

hospital revenue bond Debt issued by a city, county, state, or hospital authority with payment guaranteed by the hospital's revenues.

immunization Investing in fixed-income securities so that the target return on a portfolio is protected against changes in market rates of interest. Reduced interest income caused by falling rates of interest is offset by increased market values of bonds held in the portfolio.

income tax A tax levied on the income of an individual or business.

industrial development bond A municipal revenue bond with interest and principal guaranteed by the credit of a private business rather than the municipal entity issuing the bond.

intangible tax A tax imposed by some states and local governments on the market value of intangible assets such as stocks and bonds. Municipal bonds issued within a state are generally (but not always) exempt from that state's intangible tax.

interest dates The dates on which interest payments are made to bondholders.

interest rate risk The risk that market rates of interest will rise and result in a reduced market value for an investment asset. Long-term municipal bonds subject investors to substantial amounts of interest rate risk.

inverted scale An issue of serial bonds for which the yields on long maturities are less than the yields on short maturities.

investment company A firm that pools investors' money for purposes of diversification and professional money management. Some investment companies specialize in the purchase of tax-exempt securities.

investment-grade Pertaining to a bond that is suitable for purchase by institutions under the *prudent man* rule. Investment- grade generally implies a rating of BBB or higher by the rating agencies.

junk bond A bond with substantial uncertainty relative to the issuer's ability to meet interest and principal payments in a timely manner. Ratings of B and lower generally indicate junk-bond status.

junk muni-bond fund An investment company that invests in low-grade, tax-exempt securities. Junk muni-bond funds produce high, but uncertain yields.

legal opinion Statement of a bond counsel relative to the tax status and legal standing of a municipal bond issue.

letter of credit A promise of payment in the event that certain requirements are met. For municipal bond issues, a letter of credit adds the credit of a third party to the credit of the borrower.

liquidity risk The risk that a security will be difficult to sell without providing the buyer with an unusually favorable price. Many issues of municipal bonds subject investors to substantial amounts of liquidity risk.

load fund A mutual fund that levies a sales fee on the purchase of the firm's shares.

long bond A bond with a long period of time remaining until maturity.

management fee The money that is paid to an investment company's managers by the company's shareholders. Management fees are generally based on a percentage of the market value of the assets being managed.

marketability The ease with which a municipal bond can be bought and sold in the secondary market.

market risk The risk that an investment will fluctuate in price, thus subjecting an owner to the possibility of having to liquidate an asset at an inopportune time.

maturity date The date on which a debt obligation is to be repaid.

maturity length The length of time before a debt obligation is to be repaid.

maturity value The amount that will be paid to the holder of a debt security at maturity.

municipal bond fund A mutual fund that uses shareholder money to purchase municipal securities. Interest received from the municipal securities is passed through to shareholders of the fund.

Funds often specialize relative to the maturity length of securities or the geographic area of issuers.

municipal bond insurance A third-party guarantee that interest and principal payments from a municipal bond will be made as scheduled. Municipal bond insurance is purchased by issuers from private firms to reduce the interest rate that must be paid to sell municipal securities.

Municipal Bond Insurance Association (MBIA) A consortium of private insurance companies that guarantees interest and principal payments on municipal debt.

municipal bond unit trust An unmanaged portfolio of municipal securities. Because no buying and selling of securities occurs during the life of the trust, there is no management fee charged to investors.

municipal convertible A municipal bond that is issued at a discount and which does not make interest payments until a specified number of years following the date of issue. Once interest payments begin, the payments continue until maturity.

Municipal Securities Rulemaking Board (MSRB) A regulatory board that establishes and administers the practices of the municipal securities industry.

mutual fund An investment company that continually stands ready to sell and redeem shares. Some mutual funds charge a sales fee (load) while other funds sell shares at the net asset value. A large number of mutual funds limit their holdings to tax-exempt municipal bonds.

new issue A security issue that is being offered initially to the public. Investors who purchase municipal bonds as part of a new issue are not charged a sales commission.

no-load fund A mutual fund that sells shares to the public without charging a sales commission. Shares of a no-load fund are sold at net asset value.

noncallable Pertaining to a security that cannot be called by the issuer prior to maturity. Noncallable municipal bonds offer substantial advantages to the investor.

not rated Describing fixed income securities that have not been rated by one of the rating agencies.

offering date The date on which a new security issue is to be offered for sale.

official statement Financial and operating data that is relevant to an issue of municipal bonds. An official statement is similar to a prospectus that is issued when a private corporation sells securities to the public.

order period The time during which dealers take orders for a new security issue. In many instances an order period lasts only for a few hours.

par value The stated value of a security that is printed on the certificate. Most municipal securities have a par value of $5,000 and multiples thereof.

payment date The date on which interest will be paid to owners of a bond. There are two payment dates per year applicable to municipal bonds.

per capita debt A municipality's total debt divided by the municipality's population. Per capita debt is often used by financial analysts to analyze a municipality's ability to service its debt.

pollution control bond A revenue bond issued by a municipality for which interest and principal payment is guaranteed by a private firm that used proceeds of the bond issue to purchase pollution control equipment.

prerefunded bond A bond that has been secured by an escrow fund of U.S. government securities sufficient to meet the interest and principal obligations of the prerefunded bond.

presale order An order to purchase part of a new municipal bond issue prior to the time when certain information concerning the issue is available.

primary market The market in which new securities issues are sold. A municipal bond is sold in the primary market only one time.

private activity bond A municipal bond whose funds are used for nonessential purposes. Unless specifically exempted by the federal government, interest paid by private activity bonds is fully taxable. Certain private activity bonds pay interest that is subject to the alternative minimum tax.

project note A short-term municipal security with proceeds used to finance a federally sponsored real estate project.

public housing authority bond A tax-exempt bond issued by a public housing agency with proceeds utilized to finance low-rent housing.

public power bond A bond issued by a public power agency. Payment of interest and principal typically is guaranteed only by revenues received by the power agency.

purchasing power risk The risk that unexpected inflation will reduce the real purchasing power of an investment. The potential loss of purchasing power is one of the greatest risks faced by the owners of long-term municipal bonds.

put bond A bond that permits an investor to sell the bond back to the issuer, normally at par, prior to the bond's maturity date. Dates at which the bond can be put to the issuer are generally specified at the time the bond is issued.

rate covenant A provision of municipal revenue bonds that sets a standard for how rates will be determined on a project that the bonds are used to finance.

rating agencies Private firms that rate the debt issues of both private and public organizations. Ratings assigned by rating agencies are very important in determining the interest rates that must be paid by borrowers.

real interest rate The nominal interest rate adjusted for the existing or expected rate of inflation. A municipal bond yielding 9 percent during a period when inflation is 4 percent produces a real interest rate of 5 percent.

refund   To retire securities by utilizing funds that have been raised from the sale of a new security issue. Municipalities refund bonds when interest rates have fallen and interest expense can be reduced.

reinvestment rate   The annual rate at which cash flows can be reinvested. Investors who intend to reinvest the cash flows produced by an investment run the risk that interest rates will fall and reinvested cash will earn a return lower than expected.

resource recovery revenue bond   A bond with proceeds utilized to construct a solid waste recovery facility. Revenues generated by the facility are generally used to make interest and principal payments on the bonds.

revenue bond   Municipal debt on which interest and principal payments are guaranteed only by revenues generated by a project that the bond proceeds have been used to finance. Revenue bonds are generally of lower quality than general obligation bonds.

risk   The variability of returns from an investment. The greater the variability of returns from a particular investment, the greater the risk of owning that investment.

secondary market   The market in which securities are traded following the date of original sale. Once a municipal bond has been issued the bond must be resold in the secondary market.

serial bonds   Bonds issued under a single indenture with groups of the bonds scheduled for successive maturities. Many municipal issues contain serial bonds that provide investors with a wide choice of maturities.

settlement date   The date on which payment must be made or securities must be delivered.

short bond   A bond with a short time remaining until maturity.

small-issue bond   A municipal bond that is part of a small issue for private purposes. Interest on a small-issue bond is exempt from federal income taxation.

special assessment bond A municipal bond with interest limited to revenues from payments by those who benefitted from the funds raised by the bond.

special tax bond A municipal security with interest and principal payments limited to revenues from a special tax. A county may levy a 1 percent sales tax on motel and restaurant revenues to service debt on a bond issue that has been used to finance construction of a convention center.

split rating Pertaining to a bond that is rated differently by the rating agencies. For example, one agency may rate a bond issue AAA while another agency rates the same issue AA.

taxable municipal bond A municipal bond that pays interest taxable by the federal government. Whether a municipal bond is taxable or tax-exempt is spelled out at the time the bond is issued.

tax anticipation note (TAN) A short-term municipal obligation that is utilized to provide funding until tax revenues have been received.

tax base The resources that are available for municipal taxation. A taxing authority's tax base is important in determining the ability of the authority to service its debts.

tax-exempt money market fund A mutual fund that invests in short-term municipal securities and passes through tax-exempt income to the fund's stockholders.

term bonds Bonds that mature on a single date. Many municipal issues are comprised of both serial bonds and term bonds. The term portion of an issue normally has the longest maturity of the issue and makes up the greatest proportion of the issue.

trade date The date on which a customer order is executed.

triple tax exempt Pertaining to a municipal bond that pays interest that is exempt from federal, state, and local taxation. Because some states and most local governments do not levy an income tax, triple tax exemption is not relevant to the majority of municipal bonds.

unit investment trust An unmanaged portfolio of investments. Units of the trust are sold to investors who pay a one-time fee to acquire the units. A unit investment trust that specializes in tax-exempt securities passes through tax-exempt interest to investors.

water and sewer bond A municipal bond with proceeds used to finance the construction of water and sewer systems. Revenues from the water and sewer system are pledged against the bond's debt service requirements.

when-issued Pertaining to securities that have not yet been issued. Trading in a security frequently occurs prior to the date that the certificates for the security have been issued.

yield curve The relationship between bond yields and maturity lengths.

yield to call A bond's annualized yield (including both interest and price changes) based on the assumption that the security will be called by the issuer on the first call date.

yield to maturity A bond's annualized yield based on the assumption that the security will be held until maturity.

yield to put A bond's annual yield based on the assumption that the bond will be put to the issuer on the first put date.

zero-coupon bond A bond with no periodic interest payments but which originally is sold at a large discount from face value. Investors owning zero-coupon bonds earn income from the difference between price that is paid and the price that is received at maturity or on the date of sale.

_____

_____

_____

ABOUT THE AUTHOR

David L. Scott is Professor of Accounting and Finance at Valdosta State College, Valdosta, Georgia. Professor Scott received degrees from Purdue University and Florida State University before earning a Ph.D. at the University of Arkansas at Fayetteville. Dr. Scott was born in Rushville, Indiana, and is the author of over a dozen books including *Understanding and Managing Investment Risk and Return* in this series and *Wall Street Words* by Houghton Mifflin.